Annotated International Accounting Bibliography 1972 - 1981

Abdel M. Agami
Old Dominion University

Felix P. Kollaritsch
Ohio State University

International Accounting Section
American Accounting Association

American Accounting Association
5717 Bessie Drive
Sarasota, Florida 33583

TABLE OF CONTENTS

FOREWORD i

PREFACE ii

INTRODUCTION 1
  The Multinational Enterprise: Challenges
    and Problems 1
  The Need for International Accounting 2

FINANCIAL REPORTING PROBLEMS 4
  Consolidation of Foreign Subsidiaries 4
  Harmonization of Accounting Standards 5
  Foreign Currency Translation 14
  Accounting For Inflation in Various Countries 31
  Financial Disclosure in Various Countries 47
  Segmental Reporting 51
  Social Responsibility Disclosure in Various
    Countries 52
  International Auditing Problems 56
  The Foreign Corrupt Practices Act 61

MANAGEMENT ACCOUNTING ISSUES 65
  Challenges for Managerial Accountants 65
  Multinational Corporate Pricing 65
  Investing and Financing Decisions 66
  Financial Risk Management 79
  Political Risk Management 92
  Control and Performance Evaluation of Foreign
    Operations 94
  Transfer Pricing 97
  International Tax Planning 101

ACCOUNTING STANDARDS AND PRACTICES IN SELECTED
  COUNTRIES AND REGIONS 118
  Asia 118
  Australia and New Zealand 122
  Canada 125
  Central and South America 126
  Developing Countries 128
  Europe 132
    Belgium 132
    Denmark 133
    France 133
    Germany 134
    Greece 135
    Holland 136
    Italy 137

    Portugal 137
    Spain 137
    United Kingdom 138
  European Economic Community 140
  Middle East 146
  Non-Market Countries 149

INTERNATIONAL ACCOUNTING EDUCATION 154

AUTHOR INDEX 157

JOURNALS RESEARCHED 175

—

FOREWORD

The International Accounting Section of the American Accounting Association is pleased to sponsor the publication and distribution of Annotated International Accounting Bibliography--1972-1981. This monograph is the fifth major publication in the Section's continuing effort to encourage and facilitate international accounting education and research. The four previous books issued by the Section are:

A Compendium of Research on Information and Accounting for Managerial Decision and Control in Japan (1982), edited by Sato, Sakate, Mueller, and Radebaugh

The International Accounting and Tax Researchers' Publication Guide (1982), by Burns, Diamond, and Gernon

Eighty-Eight International Accounting Problems in Rank Order of Importance--A DELPHI Evaluation (1980), by Scott (out of print)

Notable Contributions to the Periodicals Literature-- 1975-78 (1979), edited by Selection Committee of the International Accounting Section

The project to prepare an annotated bibliography was approved in April 1982 by the Publication Committee (chaired by Lee H. Radebaugh) and the Officers of the Section (chaired by Thomas G. Evans). Authors Abdel M. Agami and Felix P. Kollaritsch are to be commended for this important contribution to the study of international accounting. Both their extensive coverage of the literature for 1972-81 and the topical organization should prove beneficial in many different ways to all of us.

It is the policy of the International Accounting Section to provide each of its members with a copy of Section sponsored publications. Additional copies are available for sale through the American Accounting Association, 5717 Bessie Drive, Saratota, Florida 33583.

Jane O. Burns, 1982-3 Chairperson
International Accounting Section
American Accounting Association

Indiana University
Indianapolis/Bloomington
Indiana

This monograph brings to your attention almost one thousand annotated articles on international accounting published in thirty-five periodicals in the USA, Australia, Canada, New Zealand, the United Kingdom, and West Germany from 1972 to 1981. We hope that you will find this monograph helpful to you in your teaching and research interests. This monograph could be used in developing or updating international accounting course assignment sheets, and in surveying literature for research. Professors who teach international accounting could also make it accessible to students to help them decide on their readings for class discussion as well as for writing term papers. Since this monograph includes a section dealing with articles that describe accounting standards and practices in selected countries and regions of the world, accounting practitioners will find this monograph of special interest to them.

The annotations were classified into one of five categories: (1) Introduction, which includes a section on challenges and problems faced by multinational enterprises, and a section dealing with the need for international accounting; (2) Financial Reporting Problems, which includes a section on consolidation of foreign subsidiaries, harmonization of accounting standards, foreign currency translation, accounting for inflation in various countries, financial disclosure in various countries, segmental reporting, social responsibility disclosure in various countries, international auditing problems, and the foreign corrupt practices act; (3) Management Accounting issues, which includes a section on challenges for managerial accountants, multinational corporate pricing, investing and financing decisions, financial risk management, political risk management, control and performance evaluation of foreign operations, transfer pricing, and international tax planning; (4) Accounting Standards and Practices in Selected Countries and Regions; and (5) International Accounting Education. Whenever an annotation was relevant to more than one section, the authors took the liberty of including it only in the section that, in their opinion, was most appropriate due to size and cost constraints. For this reason, the reader may find it worthwhile to check all related topics when searching a specific topic.

While any errors or other shortcomings of the monograph are solely the responsibility of the authors, they would like to acknowledge the encouragement and help of Professors Norlin G. Rueschhoff of Notre Dame University, Jane O. Burns of Indiana University, Thomas G. Evans of The University of South Carolina, Lee H. Radebaugh of Brigham Young University, and Michael A. Diamond of California State University Los Angeles, without which this project would never have been completed. The authors would also like to thank Professors Frederick D.S. Choi of New York University, Roger Y.W. Tang of The University of Calgary, Canada, Raj Aggarwal of The University of Toledo, S.J. Sawicki of Victoria University of Wellington, New Zealand, and many others for bringing to our attention some relevant publications.

ABDEL M. AGAMI
FELIX P. KOLLARITSCH

INTRODUCTION

The Multinational Enterprise:
Challenges and Problems

Beecroft, Kenner, Dieter Schmidt, and Stanley Weinstein. "Going International." CA Magazine, 106 (April 1975), 47-50.
The authors provide a blueprint on going international without suffering too many growing pains.

Benoit, Emile. "The Attack on the Multinationals." Columbia Journal of World Business, 7 (Nov.-Dec. 1972), 15-22.
The author believes there is no objective basis for all the criticism of and hostility towards MNCs. He believes governments should stop trying to exploit the political value of the MNC, and utilize the potential economic value.

Ewing, David W. "MNCs on Trial." Harvard Business Review, 50 (May-June 1972), 130-143.
American MNCs are beset at home by labor unions claiming that they are exporting jobs, and abroad by foreign governments claiming that they are exploiters. This article cites some of the important current literature about MNCs.

Galbraith, John Kenneth. "The Defense of the Multinational Company." Harvard Business Review, 56 (March-April 1978), 83-93.
In this article, the author looks first at the circumstances that explain the rise of the multinational corporation; next at the ideas which now guide its defense; then at the case as it might be made; and, finally, at the cautionary management behavior that this defense requires.

Kendall, Donald M. "The Need for Multinationals." Columbia Journal of World Business, 8 (Fall 1973), 103-106.
The author points out that U.S. multinationals have contributed to the U.S. balance of trade, created jobs, and promoted technological exchange. The threat to their existence, the Burke-Harke bill, must be overridden through passage of the Trade Reform Act of 1973.

Mahotiere, Stuart de la. "The Multinationals Role in a Changing World." Accountancy, 87 (March 1976), 28-33.
The author points out the contributions and problems that face multinationals in various countries. He tries to answer these questions: Do multinationals take too much and put too little back in? What is, or should be, their role? What are the special problems for the accountant?

Maisonrouge, Jacques G. "The Mythology of Multinationalism." <u>Columbia Journal of World Business</u>, 9 (Spring 1974),
7-12.
The author discusses four myths which he considers as representative of the erroneous ideas currently beclouding the
business horizon and suggests that MNCs need candor and an
aggressive effort to get their story across.

Milam, Edward E., and Gouranga Ganguli. "The Multina-
tionals--Here to Stay." <u>Financial Executive</u>, 46 (January
1978), 40-45.
The authors summarize the arguments for and against MNEs,
and conclude that MNCs are here to stay.

Robock, Stefan H. "The Case for Home Country Controls Over
Multinationals." <u>Columbia Journal of World Business</u>, 9
(Summer 1974), 75-79.
The potential for conflict exists between MNEs and nation-
states. The author makes a case for home country controls
over MNCs.

Woelfel, Charles J. "Understanding the Multinationals."
<u>The International Journal of Accounting Education and Re-
search</u>, 11 (Spring 1976), 133-142.
The observations from this study of the MNC are supported
by evidence drawn from discussions and correspondence with
executives in major MNCs and members of academia. The
author speculates on the role of the MNC in the future.

The Need for International Accounting

Benson, Sir Henry. "International Accounting: The Chal-
lenge of the Future." <u>The Journal of Accountancy</u>, 144 (No-
vember 1977), 93-96.
This article is adapted from an address by the author on
April 19, 1977, at the Ninth Annual Center Dinner of the
University of Hartford Center for the Study of Professional
Accounting.

Chastney, John G. "On to International Accounting."
<u>Accountancy</u>, 87 (July 1976), 76-80.
This essay looks at the methods by which national accounting develops, suggests why international accounting is
important, and how it can be expanded.

Enthoven, Adolf J.H. "The Unity of Accountancy in An International Context." <u>The International Journal of Accounting
Education and Research</u>, 9 (Fall 1973), 113-134.

This paper examines the various functional areas in which greater unification is needed to make the accountancy discipline a more effective instrument in the socio-economic environment.

Mueller, Gerhard G. "Accounting for Multinationals." Accountancy, 86 (July 1975), 68-75.
This article deals with the unique problems in accounting for multinational companies. Taxation, foreign currency translation, multinational transfer pricing, financial planning, multinational performance evaluation, and information systems are discussed.

Nobes, Christopher. "Why International Accounting is Important." The Accountant, 177 (8 September 1977), 277-278.
This is the first of a two-part article dealing with international accounting. A look is taken at the most important countries from the UK point of view.

Nobes, Christopher. "Why International Accounting is Important (2)." The Accountant, 177 (15 September 1977), 312-314.
This is the conclusion of a two-part article on international accounting. The author discusses the influence of taxation of accounts, and arguments for acceptance of harmonized accounting practices.

Qureshi, Mahmoud. "Pragmatic and Academic Bases of International Accounting." Management International Review, (1979/2), 61-68.
The purpose of this article is to explore the international dimensions of accounting, and its focus is on financial accounting. The discussion explores what international accounting is, and how and why we should study it.

Savoie, Leonard M. "Financial and Accounting Aspects In International Business." The International Journal of Accounting Education and Research, 9 (Fall 1973), 13-22.
The author describes the experience of his firm and how it became a MNC. Financial accounting problems are discussed.

FINANCIAL REPORTING PROBLEMS

Consolidation of Foreign Subsidiaries

Ameiss, Albert P. "Two Decades of Change in Foreign Subsidiary Accounting and United States Consolidation Practices." The International Journal of Accounting Education and Research, 7 (Spring 1972), 1-22.
This article reports the results of a survey of consolidation practices made in 1950 and repeated in 1970.

Mazzolini, Renato. "The Obstacle Course for European Transnational Consolidations." Columbia Journal of World Business, 8 (Spring 1973), 53-60.
The purpose of this article is to show that the generally perceived legal and fiscal barriers to European Transnational Consolidations are of trivial importance from the business executive's point of view.

Methven, Paul, and Chris Willows. "How RT2 Handles Multi-Currency Consolidation by Computer." Accountancy, 90 (June 1979), 101-106.
This article describes a computer system developed by RT2 for consolidating financial statement of the parent and its foreign subsidiaries.

Motekat, Ula K. "Accounting for Acquisition of Foreign Subsidiaries." The Woman CPA, 39 (April 1977), 20-22.
This article deals with the accounting problems related to acquiring a foreign subsidiary, such as the problem of determining book value and market value of the various assets and liabilities of the foreign subsidiary.

Motekat, Ula K. "The Case of the Uncontrolled Foreign Subsidiary." The Woman CPA, 39 (July 1977), 24-25.
The accounting problems of measurement and disclosure related to uncontrolled foreign subsidiaries are described.

Parker, R.H. "Concepts of Consolidation in the EEC." Accountancy, 88 (February 1977), 72-75.
The author offers a theoretical analysis of concepts of consolidation (not including so-called merger accounting) and then surveys actual practice in the UK, West Germany, France and the Netherlands.

Parker, R.H. "Explaining National Differences in Consolidated Accounts." Accounting and Business Research, 7 (Summer 1977), 203-207.
The aim of this article is to attempt an explanation of why

accounting theory and practice in relation to consolidated accounts still differ considerably from country to country, even in advanced industrial nations.

Schweikart, James A. "We Must End Consolidation of Foreign Subsidiaries." Management Accounting, 63 (August 1981), 15-25.
The author argues that a method of segment reporting that preserves domestic information must be instituted to take the place of foreign subsidiary consolidation.

Walker, R.G. "International Accounting Compromises: The Case of Consolidation Accounting." Abacus, 14 (December 1978), 97-111.
IAS 3 and the prior exposure draft are reviewed, then related to a report of the Accountants International Study Group and some national practices concerning the preparation of consolidated statements and the use of equity accounting.

Harmonization of Accounting Standards

AlHashim, Dhia D. "Accounting Control Through Purposive Uniformity: An International Perspective." The International Journal of Accounting Education and Research, 8 (Spring 1973), 21-32.
The author discusses the role of purposive uniformity in the United States, including comments on its application in Germany, France, Egypt, and Iraq, and draws inferences pertinent to accounting control in the United States.

AlHashim, Dhia D. "Regulation of Financial Accounting: An International Perspective." The International Journal of Accounting Education and Research, 16 (Fall 1980), 47-62.
The issue of regulation of financial accounting in different countries is dealt with. Financial regulations in Brazil, France, Germany, Japan, the Netherlands, Switzerland, the UK, and the US are examined.

Bartlett, Ralph T. "Current Developments of the IASC." The CPA Journal, 51 (May 1981), 20-27.
The author outlines the background of IASC, its method of operation, and gives a synopsis of its total output, in addition to its recent publications.

Belkaoui, Ahmed, Alfred Kahl, and Josette Peyrard. "Information Needs of Financial Analysts: An International Comparison." The International Journal of Accounting Education and Research, 13 (Fall 1977), 19-28.

This study tests for differences between Canadian and U.S.
financial analysts on the value of information for equity
investment decisions, and between North American and European analysts on the value for equity investment decisions.

Benson, Sir Henry. "The Story of International Accounting
Standards." Accountancy, 87 (July 1976), 34-39.
The author tells how the movement to establish international accounting standards began, and also offers some
thoughts for the future.

Brown, Jan Giannini. "The Development of International
Accounting Standards." The Woman CPA, 39 (October 1977),
9-12.
This paper examines the international accounting environment and the search for international accounting standards.

Chetkovich, Michael N. "An Appeal For Unity in Establishing
Financial Accounting Standards." The International Journal
of Accounting Education and Research, 8 (Fall 1972), 99-107.
The author endorses the recommendations of the Wheat Committee Report and also discusses the objectives of the Accounting Objectives Study Group.

Choi, Frederick D.S. "A Cluster Approach to Accounting Harmonization." Management Accounting, 63 (August 1981), 26-
31.
The author points out that steps are currently being taken
to reduce accounting diversity to harmonize global accounting standards. A cluster approach is offered.

Corbett, P. Graham. "International Accounting Standards:
The Impact on Practicising Firms." The Accountant, 176
(26 May 1977), 602-603.
The author points out that for international accounting
standards to have a real impact they must be seen to contribute to the usefulness, credibility and comprehensi-
bility of financial statements.

Corbett, P. Graham. "Why International Accounting Standards?" CA Magazine, 111 (July 1978), 36-39.
This article is based on a paper delivered at the 1977 Conference on International Accounting Standards, held in Lon-
don, England. The author exhorts accountants to begin to
apply international standards on a worldwide basis.

Cowperthwaite, Gordon H. "Prospectus for International
Harmonization." CA Magazine, 108 (June 1976), 22-31.
This article describes the background for the creation of

the International Federation of Accountants, its objectives, and how IFAC will affect IASC.

Cummings, Joseph P. "The International Accounting Standards Committee--Its Purpose and Status." The CPA Journal, 44 (September 1974), 50-53.
The author provides background and objectives for the IASC, as well as a summary of the status of IASC activities.

Cummings, Joseph P. "The International Accounting Standards Committee: Current and Future Developments." The International Journal of Accounting Education and Research, 11 (Fall 1975), 31-37.
The author examines the IASC's progress since 1973, and assesses its probable impact on the United States.

Cummings, Joseph P., and Michael N. Chetkovich. "World Accounting Enters A New Era." The Journal of Accountancy, 145 (April 1978), 52-62.
This article summarizes international accounting activities over the last decade and discusses the objectives and structure of the two international accounting bodies that will spearhead future efforts to harmonize these standards.

Cummings, Joseph P., and William L. Rogers. "Developments in International Accounting." The CPA Journal, 48 (May 1978), 15-19.
This article lists some of the international groups which have suggested international standards for reporting the results of multinationals and guidelines for their behavior, and given an update of these groups' activities.

DaCosta, Richard C., Jacques C. Bourgeois, and William M. Lawson. "A Classification of International Financial Accounting Practices." The International Journal of Accounting Education and Research, 13 (Spring 1978), 73-86.
This paper empirically investigates the existence of three financial accounting models that are alluded to in international accounting literature--the American, the British, and the continental--to which member countries adhere.

deBruyne, D. "Global Standards: A Tower of Babel?" Financial Executive, 48 (February 1980), 30-37.
The author makes a case for greater international harmonization of accounting standards and practices.

Elsea, Carole Ann. "Progress Toward International GAAP." The Woman CPA, 41 (July 1979), 22-23.
This article describes the problems encountered in the

development of international accounting standards, the progress that has taken place already, and expectations for the future.

Feldman, Stewart A., and LeRoy J. Herbert. "The International Accounting Standards Committee." The CPA Journal, 47 (January 1977), 17-21.
This article gives a description of the IASC, and a summary of its work to date.

Firth, Michael A. "An Empirical Examination of the Applicability of Adopting the AICPA and NYSE Regulations on Free Share Distribution in the U.K." Journal of Accounting Research, 11 (Spring 1973), 16-24.
The author studied the effect of adopting the American methods of accounting for stock dividends and stock split in the U.K. His aim was to undertake an investigation on the applicability of adopting American procedures in the U.K.

Fitzgerald, Richard D. "International Disclosure Standards--The United Nations Position." Journal of Accounting, Auditing, and Finance, 3 (Fall 1979), 5-20.
This article summarizes and outlines the main points introduced by the Report of the Group of Experts on International Standards of Accounting and Reporting, together with the U.N. Secretary-General's recommendations.

Fitzgerald, Richard D. "International Harmonization of Accounting and Reporting." The International Journal of Accounting Education and Research, 17 (Fall 1981), 21-32.
This paper examines the differences in accounting and reporting practices existing in various parts of the world, the problems which these differences cause, and the efforts that are being made to mitigate the differences.

Gaertner, James F., and Norlin Rueschhoff. "Cultural Barriers to International Accounting Standards." CA Magazine, 113 (May 1980), 36-39.
The authors illustrate some of the cultural, economic, and social differences between countries, and how they affect accounting.

Gray, S.J. "Multinational Enterprises and the Development of International Accounting Standards." The Chartered Accountant in Australia, 52 (August 1981), 24-25.
The author outlines major issues and trends relating to the development of international accounting standards and the accountability of multinational enterprises.

Gray, S.J. "The Impact of International Accounting Differences from a Security-Analysis Perspective: Some European Evidence." Journal of Accounting Research, 18 (Spring 1980), 64-76.
This paper empirically explores the question of impact and the extent to which the measurement of company profits is correlated with national characteristics.

Hampton, Robert III. "World of Difference in Accounting and Reporting." Management Accounting, 62 (September 1980), 14-18.
Reasons for differences in accounting practices and standards in different countries are explained. The article also points out the need for harmonization, and summarizes the contributions made toward that goal to date.

Harvey, Iain. "International Standards--Why We Need Them." Accountancy, 88 (March 1977), 96-98.
The author considers merits of international Standards and argues that accountants should support their development.

Hauworth, William P. "Problems in the Development of Worldwide Accounting Standards." The International Journal of Accounting Education and Research, 9 (Fall 1973), 23-34.
The author outlines and analyzes factors creating differences in accounting standards and practices in the world. He also explains the factors that might help in accelerating the development of worldwide accounting standards.

Hayes, Donald J. "The International Accounting Standards Committee--Recent Developments and Current Problems." The International Journal of Accounting Education and Research, 16 (Fall 1980), 1-10.
This paper discusses some of the problems facing the IASC, how the author believes IASC should react to them, and some of its recent accomplishments.

Howe, Wong Eng. "International Standards of Accounting and Reporting." The Australian Accountant, 50 (August 1980), 435-440.
This article reviews United Nations action towards establishing an international, comparable system of standardized accounting and reporting.

Hussein, Mohamed Elmutassim. "Translation Problems of International Standards." The International Journal of Accounting Education and Research, 17 (Fall 1981), 147-156.
This article points out the problems encountered in translating IASC standards. The author proposes using the back-

translation method to ensure that the translation corresponds to the original English.

Kanaga, William. "International Accounting: The Challenge and the Changes." The Journal of Accountancy, 150 (November 1980), 55-61.
The chairman of the AICPA discusses some current problems of international practice and explains why he is optimistic that the profession will eventually achieve harmonization of international accounting and auditing standards.

Kewin, A.H.E. "I.A.S. 4--Depreciation Accounting: A Comparison with the Australian Standard." The Australian Accountant, 46 (October 1976), 555-556.
The author compares the International Standard (issued in 1976) with the Australian Standard issued in 1974.

Lamond, Robert A. "The Role of the International Practices Committee." The Chartered Accountant in Australia, 49 (March 1979), 12-14.
The author, Australia's representative on this International Federation of Accountants (IFAC) Committee, explains its role and outlines its future program.

Mason, Alister K. "International Reporting of Inventories: Potential Impact of IAS 2." The Accountant, 174 (7 October 1976), 410-413.
The author seeks to analyse the potential impact of IAS 2. The analysis includes 23 countries, many of which are very important from an economic standpoint.

McComb, Desmond. "The International Harmonization of Accounting: A Cultural Dimension." The International Journal of Accounting Education and Research, 14 (Spring 1979), 1-16.
The author examines the conceptual justification for national differences in accounting standards and practices. He concludes that emphasis should be upon investigation, analysis, and education rather than speeding the processes of promulgating further international accounting standards.

McKenzie, Alec. "The Progress of the International Accounting Standards Committee: The First Two Years." The Accountant's Magazine, 80 (April 1976), 137-139.
The author presents his views on the progress of the IASC towards greater harmonization of accounting standards.

McMonnies, P.N. "EEC, UEC, ASC, IASC, IASG, AISG, ICCAP, IFAC, Old Uncle Tom Cobbleigh and All." Accounting and

Business Research, 7 (Summer 1977), 162-167.
This paper is a critique of the present rule-making scene.

Miles, J.N. "The Development of International Accounting
Standards." The Chartered Accountant in Australia, 49
(August 1978), 26-32.
The purpose of this paper is to consider the criteria for
the establishment of effective accounting standards, to
trace the development of international accounting standards,
and to review the standards so far issued by the IASC.

Miles, J.N. "The Development of International Accounting
Standards Part 2." The Chartered Accountant in Australia,
49 (September 1978), 33-37.
This is the conclusion of a paper presented by the author
at the Singapore/Australia Accountants Seminar. Part I
appeared in the August issue.

Mueller, G.G. "International Accounting Standards and Problems." The Accountant, 177 (13 October 1977), 446-449.
The author exhorts the profession to respond to the challenges of international accounting before governments find
it necessary to impose regulations.

Mueller, Gerhard G., and Lauren M. Walker. "The Coming of
Age of Financial Transnational Reporting." The Journal of
Accountancy, 142 (July 1976), 67-74.
The authors discuss three approaches to the problem of
transnational financial reporting and conclude that, with
the aid of the IASC, internationally accepted accounting
standards will be achieved in the future.

Nair, R.D., and Werner G. Frank. "The Harmonization of International Accounting Standards, 1973-79." The International Journal of Accounting Education and Research, 17
(Fall 1981), 61-78.
This study isolates those practices on which progress towards harmonization has been made, relates them to the pronouncements of the IASC, and examines which countries have
made changes regarding those accounting practices.

Nair, R.D., and Werner G. Frank. "The Impact of Disclosure
and Measurement Practices on International Accounting."
The Accounting Review, 55 (July 1980), 426-450.
This article examines whether the classification of countries into groups based on their accounting practices is
the same whether measurement or disclosure practices are
used to do the groupings.

Needles, Belverd E., Jr. "Implementing a Framework for the International Transfer of Accounting Technology." The International Journal of Accounting Education and Research, 12 (Fall 1976), 45-62.
A conceptual framework by which a country may formulate a strategy for international transfer of accounting technology as part of its overall economic plan is proposed.

Nobes, C.W. "An Empirical Analysis of International Accounting Principles: A Comment." Journal of Accounting Research, 19 (Spring 1981), 268-270.
This is a comment on Werner G. Frank's article entitled, "An Empirical Analysis of International Accounting Principles," published in this journal (Autumn 1979).

Owles, Derrick. "Foreign Affairs--International Harmonization." The Accountant Annual Review 1979-1980 (Supplement to The Accountant), 182 (3 April 1980), 4-6.
The purpose of this article is to summarize the work being done by the various national and international bodies towards the process of harmonization.

Pomeranz, Felix. "Prospects for International Accounting and Auditing Standards--The Transnationals in Governmental Regulations." The International Journal of Accounting Education and Research, 17 (Fall 1981), 7-20.
This paper presents some reasons for differences in accounting principles, reports the status of accounting rule-making, and offers suggestions.

Previts, Gary John. "On the Subject of Methodology and Models for International Accountancy." The International Journal of Accounting Education and Research, 10 (Spring 1975), 1-12.
This paper focuses upon the matter of methodology for reviewing and synthesizing global accounting developments, considering interrelationships which have arisen from the changing economic and financial environment.

Schieneman, Gary S. "International Accounting: Issues and Perspective." Journal of Accounting, Auditing, and Finance, 3 (Fall 1979), 21-30.
This article examines the proposition that more harmonization of international accounting standards would overcome the reporting problems faced by multinationals, and discusses some reasons why more uniformity in international accounting has not been achieved at the present time. It then looks at possible future developments in this area.

Schwartz, Ivo. "The Harmonization of Accounting and Auditing in the European Community." The Accountant's Magazine, 81 (December 1977), 508-510.
This article is concerned with the subject of harmonization from the point of view of the European community.

Smith, Willis A. "International Accounting Standards—An Update." The CPA Journal, 50 (June 1980), 22-27.
The author describes the work of a number of international organizations, among them UN, OECD, EEC, AFA, AAC, IFAC, and IASC, that are working on accounting standards with the objective of worldwide harmonization.

Stillwell, M.I. "'Generally Accepted Accounting Principles...': Why the Americans Report as they Do." The Accountant, 175 (25 November 1976), 607-608.
The author outlines the legal and historical influences on the development of "generally accepted accounting principles" in the United States.

Thomas, R.D. "The Closer We Get the Better We'll Look." The Australian Accountant, 46 (August 1976), 400-404.
The importance of harmonizing accounting standards, with special reference to the role and work of the Accountants International Study Group and the International Accounting Standards Committee, is emphasized.

Vincent, Geoff. "Australia's International Involvement." The Australian Accountant, 50 (August 1980), 441-448.
The author outlines the background of the IFAC, the IASC, and the CAPA, where they stand on matters affecting accountants around the world, and some of the current proposals for the future of such bodies.

Vincent, Geoff. "Towards International Standards for Accountants." The Australian Accountant, 51 (March 1981), 98-99.
The author reviews the work of the IASC toward developing methods for harmonizing world standards for accountants.

Watt, George C. "Toward Worldwide Accounting Principles." The CPA Journal, 42 (August 1972), 651-653.
This article outlines efforts made toward developing worldwide accounting principles since the Ninth International Congress of Accountants in 1967, and indicates significant areas for attention in the five years beginning in 1972.

Abs, Hermann J. "Bretton Woods: Temporarily Suspended or Obsolete?" Columbia Journal of World Business, 7 (January-February 1972), 7-12.
The author discusses reasons for the breakdown of the international monetary system, and advocates a return to fixed exchange rates.

Agami, Abdel M., and Ula K. Motekat. "The Proposed Statement On Foreign Currency Translation." The Woman CPA, 43 (January 1981), 23-26.
This article explains and illustrates provisions of the Proposed Statement of Financial Accounting Standard on foreign currency translation issued in August 1980, and highlights major differences between it and Statement No. 8.

Aggarwal, Raj. "The Translation Problem in International Accounting: Insights for Financial Management." Management International Review, 15 (1975/2-3), 67-79.
This paper examines the problems in the use of currently available accounting procedures for the translation and consolidation of foreign subsidiary financial statements from the viewpoint of the financial manager of a MNC.

Aggarwal, Raj, and James C. Baker. "Using Foreign Subsidiary Accounting Data: A Dilemma for the Multinational Corporation." Columbia Journal of World Business, 10 (Fall 1975), 83-92.
The earning power principle is introduced as a method for more accurately translating foreign subsidiary financial statements.

Aggarwal, Raj. "Analyzing Multinational Company Financial Statements: Role of the New Accounts Translation Standard." Southern Business Review, 4 (Spring 1976), 1-10.
The influence of FASB #8 on reported financial statements of U.S.-based MNCs is examined. The new translation method is compared to other, previously used, methods in its effect both on the balance sheets and the reported earnings.

Aggarwal, Raj. "FASB No. 8 and Reported Results of Multinational Operations: Hazard for Managers and Investors." Journal of Accounting, Auditing and Finance, 1 (Spring 1978), 197-216.
The author examines the translation process and the effect of FASB No. 8 on reported financial statements, and spotlights operating and accounting changes--and attendant problems--induced in MNCs by its use.

14

Aliber, Robert Z., and Clyde P. Stickney. "Accounting Measures of Foreign Exchange Exposure." The Accounting Review, 50 (January 1975), 44-57.
This article asserts that assumptions regarding exposure to exchange losses implied in current accounting methodology for translating foreign financial statements into dollars are logically inconsistent and empirically unjustifiable.

Aliber, Robert Z. "Monetary Interdependence Under Floating Exchange Rates." The Journal of Finance, 30 (May 1975), 365-376.
This paper examines whether the major advantages attributed to floating rates have been achieved.

Armstrong-Flemming, Nigel. "Multicurrency Accounting: Dispelling the Mystique." Accountancy, 92 (March 1981), 118-120.
The purposes of this article are to suggest why and when to use multicurrency accounting, to explain briefly the techniques involved in keeping multicurrency accounting records, and to discuss the advantages and disadvantages.

Barrett, M.E., and L. Spero. "Foreign Exchange Gains and Losses." Financial Analysts Journal, 31 (March/April 1975), 26-31.
The authors identify three factors governing the impact of exchange gains and losses on statements, and discuss them in the context of both British and American practice.

Benjamin, James J., and Steven D. Grossman. "Foreign Currency Translation: An Update." The CPA Journal, 51 (February 1981), 48-52.
The authors describe practices used in recent years for translation into US currency of items and statements in foreign currencies, the rules propounded in FASB 8, and the proposal of the Board in its current exposure draft.

Bilson, John F.O. "Leading Indicators of Currency Devaluation." Columbia Journal of World Business, 14 (Winter 1979), 62-76.
The author rejects relative inflation rates "purchasing parity" as a predictor of currency changes. Instead he provides a simple monetary model as a leading indicator of devaluations in countries with exchange controls.

Bradford, Samuel R. "Exchange Rates--Factors Determining Trends." Accountancy, 87 (May 1976), 44-46.
The author looks at some of the more important factors determining currency relationships.

Brittain, W.H. Bruce. "Have Flexible Exchange Rates
Caused World Inflation?" Columbia Journal of World Business, 10 (Fall 1975), 101-105.
The author explains how the world's inflation problems were
caused by perverse monetary policies rather than a perverse
exchange rate regime.

Burt, John, Fred R. Kaen, and G. Geoffrey Booth. "Foreign
Exchange Market Efficiency Under Flexible Exchange Rates."
The Journal of Finance, 32 (September 1977), 1325-1330.
This paper presents an empirical analysis of spot exchange
rate behavior subsequent to the decision in 1973 by major
central banks of Western Europe to abandon dollar support
of their currencies within fixed intervention points.

Burt, John, Fred R. Kaen, and G. Geoffrey Booth. "Foreign
Exchange Market Efficiency Under Flexible Exchange Rates:
A Reply." The Journal of Finance, 34 (June 1979), 791-793.
The authors defend their original article which appeared in
the September 1977 issue of The Journal of Finance. The
results of their research were questioned by Miles and
Wilford in this June 1979 issue.

Carstairs, Ralph. "Accounting and Management Aspects of
Foreign Exchange Transactions." The Australian Accountant,
49 (August 1979), 454-464, 493.
This article deals with the accounting for foreign exchange
transaction and translation, the mechanics of the foreign
exchange market in Australia, and the management of foreign
exchange exposure.

Choi, Frederick D.S. "Price-Level Adjustments and Foreign
Currency Translations: Are They Compatible?" The International Journal of Accounting Education and Research, 11
(Fall 1975), 121-143.
The restate-translate versus translate-restate controversy
is viewed along with arguments supporting each model. Conclusions, insights, and policy implications are given.

Choi, Frederick D.S., Howard D. Lowe, and Reginald G.
Worthley. "Accountors, Accountants, and Standard No. 8."
Journal of International Business Studies, 9 (Fall 1978),
81-87.
This article surveys the reactions of financial executives
(accountors) and professional accountants to the FASB's
recent pronouncement on foreign currency translation.

Christofides, N., R.D. Hewins, and G.R. Salkin. "Graphic
Theoretic Approaches to Foreign Exchange." Journal of

Financial and Quantitative Analysis, 14 (September 1979), 481-500.
This paper explains the different kinds of arbitrages that exist in foreign currency exchange dealing and provides graphic theoretic formulations for the various types.

Clark, F.L. "Patz on Parities, Exchange Rates and Translation." Accounting and Business Research, 9 (Winter 1978), 73-77.
This is a comment on Professor Patz's article in the Winter 1977 issue of Accounting and Business Research.

Combes, J.H., and J.W. Houghton. "Translating Foreign Currency." Financial Executive, 41 (December 1973), 8-16.
The authors report the results of a survey of the year-end foreign translation practices of 45 "Fortune 500" U.S.-based multinational companies.

Connor, Joseph E. "Accounting for the Upward Float in Foreign Currencies." The Journal of Accountancy, 133 (June 1972), 39-44.
The author discusses two established exchange methods--current/noncurrent and monetary/nonmonetary--and proposes the use of the current rate method which he believes indicates the economic facts more closely than the other two.

Cooper, J.R.H. "Foreign Exchange Operations." Accountancy, 85 (August 1974), 54-58.
The author highlights the problems that arise when foreign exchange operations go wrong.

Cooper, Kerry, Donald R. Fraser, and R. Malcolm Richards. "The Impact of SFAS #8 on Financial Management Practices." Financial Executive, 46 (June 1978), 26-31.
This article reports the results of a survey of financial executives dealing with changes in management practices or procedures that firms might have employed to counter potential adverse effects of SFAS #8 on financial statements.

Copeland, Ronald M., and Robert W. Ingram. "An Evaluation of Accounting Alternatives for Foreign Currency Transactions." The International Journal of Accounting Education and Research, 13 (Spring 1978), 15-27.
This paper reviews the theoretical basis for the requirements promulgated by the FASB and empirically tests their validity in light of economic reality.

Cornell, Bradford. "The Denomination of Foreign Trade Contracts Once Again." Journal of Financial and Quantitative

Analysis, 15 (November 1980), 933-945.
The author shows that the currency denomination problem
cannot be analyzed without considering the source of exchange rate variation. An integrated interpretative model
and some preliminary empirical results are presented.

Cornell, Bradford, and Marc R. Reinganum. "Forward and Future Prices: Evidence From the Foreign Exchange Markets."
The Journal of Finance, 36 (December 1981), 1035-1046.
This paper examines the forward and futures prices in
foreign exchange in an attempt to distinguish between the
competing explanations.

Cumby, Robert E., and Maurice Obstfeld. "A Note On Exchange-Rate Expectations and Optimal Interest Differentials: A Test of the Fisher Hypothesis." The Journal of
Finance, 36 (June 1981), 697-704.
This paper tests the hypothesis that nominal interest differentials between similar assets denominated in different
currencies can be explained entirely by the expected change
in the exchange rate over the holding period.

Denis, Jack. "How Well Does the International Monetary
Market Track the Interbank Forward Market?" Financial
Analysts Journal, 32 (January/February 1976), 50-54.
This article examines changes that have happened recently
in the international monetary markets as a result of the
floating currency system and increase in size of hedging
transactions.

Deupree, Marvin M. "Translating Foreign Currency Financial
Statements." Financial Executive, 40 (October 1972), 48-68.
The author examines the questions of which exchange rates
should be applied to several types of accounts to effect
translations, and how the effects of translation adjustments
should be accounted for.

Deupree, Marvin M. "Is FASB #8 The Best Approach." Financial Executive, 46 (January 1978), 24-29.
The author examines the conceptual basis for FASB #8 and
recommends an approach toward developing a better solution
for foreign currency translation.

Duangploy, Orapin. "The Sensitivity of Earnings Per Share
to Different Foreign Currency Translation Methods." The
International Journal of Accounting Education and Research,
14 (Spring 1979), 121-134.
The purpose of this study is to determine whether the
criticism of the expected effect of the temporal method on

earnings per share is justifiable.

Earl, Michael, and Dean Paxson. "Value Accounting for Currency Transactions." Accounting and Business Research, 8 (Spring 1978), 92-100.
The authors propose and explain a system of value accounting based on the use of forward rates for recording currency transactions at transaction date.

Evans, Thomas G. "Diversity in Foreign Currency Translation Methods--A Proposal for Uniformity." The CPA Journal, 44 (February 1974), 41-45.
This article reviews the alternative translation methods in existence, presents the results of a survey about which methods are being followed in practice, and proposes the adoption of a uniform method of currency translation.

Evans, Thomas G. "Foreign Currency Translation Abroad." The CPA Journal, 44 (June 1974), 47-50.
This article reports the results of surveying 23 foreign-based corporations to discover what foreign currency translation practices were used in the preparation of consolidated financial statements and also what treatment was given to translation losses or gains.

Evans, Thomas G., and William R. Folks, Jr. "SFAS No. 8: Conforming, Coping, Complaining, and Correcting." The International Journal of Accounting Education and Research, 15 (Fall 1979), 33-43.
This paper examines SFAS No. 8 and the response it evoked in MNCs. It is based on the authors' research study published by the FASB and relies upon the questionnaire response of 156 US-based MNCs.

Fantl, Irving L. "The FASB Currency Translation Bungle." The Woman CPA, 37 (October 1975), 5-7.
The author discusses the implications of the FASB's exposure draft on foreign currency translation.

Fantl, Irving L. "Problems With Currency Translation--A Report on FASB No. 8." Financial Executive, 47 (December 1979), 33-37.
This article reports the findings of a survey questionnaire that was sent to 78 multinational firms as to the effect of Statement No. 8 on the corporation financial statements and corporation satisfaction with these results.

Fekrat, M.A. "Multinational Accounting: A Technical Note." The International Journal of Accounting Education and

Research, 15 (Fall 1979), 95-103.
Restating foreign currency financial statements in terms of
a common currency equivalent is crucial for providing a global view of the operations of multinational enterprises.
This article outlines an alternative to translation based
on a classical economic concept.

Fieleke, Norman S. "Exchange-Rate Flexibility and the Efficiency of the Foreign-Exchange Markets." Journal of Financial and Quantitative Analysis, 10 (September 1975),
409-428.
The author examines the question of whether foreign-
exchange markets function as efficiently with a high degree of flexibility as with the relatively fixed rates of
the Bretton Woods system.

Flower, John. "A Price Parity Theory of Translation: A
Comment." Accounting and Business Research, 9 (Winter
1978), 64-65.
This is a comment on Professor Patz's article in the Winter
1977 issue of Accounting and Business Research.

Fredrikson, E. Bruce. "The Valuation of Noncurrent Foreign
Currency Monetary Claims." The International Journal of
Accounting Education and Research, 9 (Fall 1973), 149-158.
This paper considers the valuation of noncurrent foreign
currency receivables and payables. It employs current interest and exchange rates to obtain a present value in the
reference currency.

Frenkel, Jacob A. "The Efficiency and Volatility of Exchange Rates and Prices in the 1970s." Columbia Journal
of World Business, 14 (Winter 1979), 15-27.
The author examines data on the volatility of exchange rates
and shows that high variability is an intrinsic characteris-
tic of this market and other asset markets where prices are
dominated by changing expectations; hence volatility is
consistent with efficiency.

Garman, Mark B., and Steven W. Kohlhagen. "Inflation and
Foreign Exchange Rates under Production and Monetary Uncertainty." Journal of Financial and Quantitative Analysis,
15 (November 1980), 949-967.
The authors apply the techniques of continuous-time con-
tingent pricing theory to the foreign exchange market.

Giddy, Ian H., and Gunter Dufey. "The Random Behavior of
the Flexible Exchange Rates: Implications for Forecasting."
Journal of International Business Studies, 6 (Spring 1975),

1-32.
This article explores the forecasting accuracy of the "random walk" and other models of exchange rate behavior. The authors present results consistent with the notion that the foreign exchange market is an "efficient market" and exchange rate forecasting is not profitable.

Giddy, Ian H. "An Integrated Theory of Exchange Rate Equilibrium." Journal of Financial and Quantitative Analysis, 11 (December 1976), 883-892.
Along with other conclusions, this paper shows that a theoretical equilibrium state of the world exists in the absence of capital controls and trade barriers.

Giddy, Ian H. "Research on the Foreign Exchange Markets." Columbia Journal of World Business, 14 (Winter 1979), 4-6.
The approach towards research on the foreign exchange markets has shifted dramatically during the 1970s. The author introduces this special issue of this journal that presents a selection of articles representing the latest thinking on the subject.

Gray, John Y. "Translating Foreign Currency Transactions and Financial Statements." The CPA Journal, 47 (June 1977), 31-36.
This article explains the provisions and requirements of the controversial FASB No. 8, and summarizes opposing reactions.

Hayes, Donald J. "Translating Foreign Currencies." Harvard Business Review, 50 (January-February 1972), 6-18, 158-159.
Until accounting rules covering new conditions can be formulated, the author believes the financial executive must weigh the guidelines on revalued currencies that do exist against his judgment and his company's situation.

Hilliard, Jimmy E. "The Relationship Between Equity Indices on World Exchanges." The Journal of Finance, 34 (March 1979), 103-114.
This paper examines the structure of international equity market indices during a world-wide financial crisis, July 7, 1973 to April 30, 1974.

Hinton, P. Raymond. "Foreign Currency Transactions." The Accountant, 178 (4 May 1978), 591-592.
This article is concerned with ED 21. The author states that he would like to see the new standard clearly identify the objective of consolidated financial statements.

Houghton, John W., Jr. "Foreign Long-Term Debt Translation." Management Accounting, 56 (September 1974), 17-18. Depending upon which accounting method is followed, foreign long-term debt may be translated into U.S. dollars at either current or historical exchange rates. However, according to the author, until valuation concepts are accepted, the fair presentation of long-term debt is elusive.

Huang, Roger D. "The Monetary Approach to Exchange Rate in An Efficient Foreign Exchange Market: Tests Based On Volatility." The Journal of Finance, 36 (March 1981), 31-42. This article shows that the variance bounds on exchange rate movements implied by monetary approach to exchange rate in efficient exchange markets is violated. Evidence also shows that forecast errors implied by the monetary model can be forecasted using historical data.

Jackson, Peter D., and Michael B. Meagher. "The New Foreign Currency Recommendations." CA Magazine, 111 (December 1978), 47-53. This article concentrates on accounting for noncurrent monetary assets and liabilities that are denominated in a foreign currency and have a fixed or ascertainable life. The authors use long term foreign debt in their example.

Jacobi, Michael H. "The Unit of Account in Consolidated Financial Statements of Multinational Enterprises." The International Journal of Accounting Education and Research, 15 (Spring 1980), 17-34. The author suggests the use of Special Drawing Rights (SDR) as the unit of account for consolidated financial statements of multinational enterprises.

Jansz, Rodney. "Foreign Currency Translation." The Australian Accountant, 51 (February 1981), 18-21. The scope of this article is restricted to translation exposure. The author describes methods of translation, and accounting treatment of translation gains or losses.

Johnson, Harry G. "The International Monetary Crisis of 1971." The Journal of Business, 46 (January 1973), 11-23. The author provides an analysis of the international monetary crisis of 1971 by viewing it in the context of the general theory of international monetary organization and the broad historical evolution of the international monetary system in contemporary times.

Klein, Richard B. "Inter-Country Purchasing Power Index Numbers." Management Accounting, 54 (August 1972), 28-32.

The author believes a more favorable picture of foreign operations would be obtained by valuing assets in terms of a translation rate based on purchasing power rather than the legal exchange rate.

Kohlhagen, Steven W. "The Performance of the Foreign Exchange Markets: 1971-1974." Journal of International Business Studies, 6 (Fall 1975), 33-40.
This paper explores the behavior of the foreign exchange markets for the floating rate period since 1973, and the immediately preceding fixed rate period.

Konrath, Larry F. "Foreign Exchange Versus Purchasing Power Gains and Losses." Management Accounting, 53 (May 1972), 41-43.
The author points out that both the official exchange rate (before and after devaluation) and inflationary aspects of each currency must be considered before deciding whether or not to convert the earnings of a subsidiary.

Leighton, G.R. "Exchange Control in Australia." The Australian Accountant, 46 (November 1976), 600-612.
The author discusses the background and legal basis, objective, regulations, general policy, aspects of current policy and administration of exchange control in Australia.

Leighton, G.R. "Exchange Control in Australia 1980." The Australian Accountant, 50 (August 1980), 465-471.
This article is based on an address given by the author at the Reserve Bank of Australia, Perth, in May of 1980. The author gives a guide to regulations governing international business and investment transactions.

Leo, K., and G. Grundy. "Foreign Currency Translation-- The Key Issues." The Chartered Accountant in Australia, 50 (February 1080), 23-28.
This article deals with the Exposure Draft "Translation of Foreign Currency Transactions and Foreign Currency Financial Statements in the Context of Historical Cost Accounting," issued by the Australian Accounting Research Foundation in June of 1979. The authors propose use of the temporal method for translating foreign financial statements. They believe that major revisions should be made to the draft.

Lewis, Kenneth A., and Francis F. Breen. "Empirical Issues in the Demand for Currency: A Multinational Study." The Journal of Finance, 30 (September 1975), 1065-1079.
Dynamic demand-for-currency functions are estimated for 24 countries with postwar annual data. International data are

used to provide independent information about currency elas-
ticities.

Lorensen, Leonard. "The Temporal Principle of Translation."
The Journal of Accountancy, 134 (August 1972), 48-54.
The author of Accounting Research Study No. 12 entitled,
"Reporting Foreign Operations of U.S. Companies in U.S. Dol-
lars," explains the temporal principle of translation.

Lorensen, Leonard. "Misconceptions About Translation." CA
Magazine, 102 (March 1973), 20-25.
The author points out that the study on translation by the
Canadian Institute of Chartered Accountants contains some
misconceptions.

Makin, John H. "Fixed Versus Floating: A Red Herring."
Columbia Journal of World Business, 14 (Winter 1979), 7-14.
Whether or not a country has fixed exchange rates, the author argues, it is subject to the influence of foreign monetary and economic policies.

Mathur, Ike, and David Loy. "Foreign Currency Translation:
Survey of Corporate Treasurers." Management Accounting, 63
(September 1981), 33-42.
The authors discuss the major issues involved in the dispute over the draft and FASB No. 8 approaches to foreign
currency translation, and report the opinions of corporate
treasurers obtained from a survey of 300 U.S. MNCs.

McMonnies, Peter N., and Bryan J. Rankin. "Accounting for
Foreign Currency Translation." The Accountant's Magazine,
81 (June 1977), 241-243.
This article describes the foreign currency translation
methods currently in use in the UK and the USA. It is the
first of a two-part article.

McMonnies, Peter N., and Bryan J. Rankin. "Accounting for
Foreign Currency Translation--II." The Accountant's Magazine, 81 (July 1977), 285-288.
This is the conclusion of a two-part article on foreign currency translation methods in use in the UK and the USA. It
examines the effect on UK accounts of the lack of a UK standard, and considers areas any new standard should cover.

McMonnies, Peter N., and Bryan J. Rankin. "Accounting for
Foreign Currency Translation--III: ED 21." The Accountant's Magazine, 81 (November 1977), 460-461.
This article summarizes the Accounting Standards Committee's
proposals on foreign currency translation, and compares them

with approaches discussed in a previous two-part article and with a Canadian Institute exposure draft.

McMonnies, Peter N., and Bryan J. Rankin. "Accounting for Foreign Currency Translation--IV: IASE 11." The Accountant's Magazine, 82 (January 1978), 16-17.
E 11 has now been published (The Accountant's Magazine December 1977), and this brief article reviews it, explaining why it leaves the authors dissatisfied.

Mensah, Yaw M., and Louis F. Biagioni. "The Predictive Ability of Financial Ratios Using Alternative Translation Methods for Foreign-Currency Financial Statements: A Simulation Study." The International Journal of Accounting Education and Research, 16 (Fall 1980), 221-245.
This study investigates whether, under certain assumptions or conditions, different translation methods will result in significantly different measures of financial ratios and which ratios can then be used to distinguish between "successful" and "non-successful" foreign subsidiaries.

Messier, William F., Jr. "SFAS No. 8: Some Implications for MNCs." The International Journal of Accounting Education and Research, 14 (Spring 1979), 101-120.
This article briefly reviews accounting practices prior to SFAS No. 8, discusses the reasons behind the new rule and explains its implementation, and examines some of the implications of SFAS No. 8 for MNCs.

Miles, Marc A., and D. Sykes Wilford. "Foreign Exchange Market Efficiency Under Flexible Exchange Rates: A Comment." The Journal of Finance, 34 (June 1979), 787-789.
The authors offer an alternative and more general explanation for the results obtained by Burt, Kaen and Booth in an article which appeared in the September 1977 issue of The Journal of Finance.

Munter, Paul. "Currency Strategies Under FASB 8: An Empirical Analysis." The International Tax Journal, 6 (December 1979), 85-95.
This article deals with the change in currency strategies for foreign subsidiaries since FASB 8 became effective to minimize its effect on the consolidated financial statements, and the use of different strategies for foreign subsidiaries in weak currency countries than for foreign subsidiaries in strong currency countries.

Nobes, C.W. "A Review of the Translation Debate." Accounting and Business Research, 10 (Autumn 1980), 421-431.

This article tries to clarify the differences in translation methods, and their causes. The author hopes to make clear how the various issues in the translation debate are connected, and how and why writers differ.

Norr, David. "Currency Translation and the Analyst." Financial Analysts Journal, 32 (July/August 1976), 46-54.
Various provisions of Statement No. 8 related to foreign currency translation are explained and illustrated.

Pakkala, A.L. "Accounting of Multinational Companies." Financial Analysts Journal, 31 (March/April 1975), 32-41.
This article analyzes the accounting options available to and used by specific firms with respect to the translation of their income statement and balance sheet.

Parkinson, R. MacDonald. "Whose Misconceptions." CA Magazine, 102 (March 1973), 26-29.
The author replies to the charges levelled by Leonard Lorensen against his Study on Translation sponsored by the Canadian Institute of Chartered Accountants.

Patz, Dennis H. "The State of the Art in Translation Theory." Journal of Business Finance & Accounting, 4 (Autumn 1977), 311-325.
The purpose of this paper is to provide a broad theoretical perspective to the problem of translating foreign accounts, to provide a theoretical specification of the state of the art in translation as a guide to future research.

Patz, Dennis H. "A Price Parity Theory of Translation." Accounting and Business Research, 8 (Winter 1977), 14-24.
This article seeks to present an explicitly stated analysis of the translation problem, and to interpret the results of this analysis in terms of fundamental concepts which provide a foundation for a price parity theory of translation.

Patz, Dennis. "A Price Parity Theory Translation: A Reply." Accounting and Business Research, 9 (Winter 1978), 66-72.
This is Professor Patz's reply to Professor Flower's comments appearing in the same issue.

Patz, D.H. "Price Parity Translation: Methodology and Implementation." Accounting and Business Research, 11 (Summer 1981), 207-216.
A specification of price parity translation methodology is presented, and consideration is given to the question of obtaining/developing reasonably accurate measures of price

parity.

Piper, Andrew. "Accounting for Overseas Currencies." The International Journal of Accounting Education and Research, 12 (Fall 1976), 63-90.
This paper seeks to introduce, describe and discuss some examples of accounting for overseas currency transactions and translations from the published accounts of companies whose registered offices are in the UK.

Piper, Andrew G. "A Note On Translation for Interim Accounts." The International Journal of Accounting Education and Research, 15 (Fall 1979), 46-52.
This paper discusses the proper method of translation for interim reports. The author concludes that investors are interested in accounts and dividends and share prices in their own currency, which would suggest that the use of closing rates at the interim reporting stage is desirable.

Pleak, Ruth E. "An Analysis of the FASB's Treatment of Foreign Currency Translation." Management Accounting, 59 (September 1977), 29-32.
The author examines FASB's Statement No. 8 dealing with foreign currency translation, the arguments the FASB used to support its choices, and some of the effects the choices have had on businesses.

Polimeni, Ralph S. "Accounting for Forward Exchange Contracts." The International Journal of Accounting Education and Research, 13 (Fall 1977), 159-168.
The purpose of this article is to provide four illustrations of the accounting for forward exchange contracts.

Portington, Michael. "Foreign Currency Translation: The New Accounting Approach." Accountancy, 92 (February 1981), 105-107.
This article discusses ED 27, a step in the development of a UK Standard for foreign currency translation. The author reports it is in harmony with US and Canadian proposals.

Price, Claudia I. "The Multinational Corporation and SFAS No. 8." The Woman CPA, 42 (October 1980), 26-30.
This article analyzes the provisions of SFAS No. 8, especially those related to exchange gains and losses and their impact on financial managers. It also proposes ways of improving the accounting for foreign currency translation.

Radebaugh, Lee. "Accounting for Price-Level and Exchange-Rate Changes for U.S. International Firms: An Empirical

Study." Journal of International Business Studies, 5 (Fall 1974), 41-56.
This article reports the result of a questionnaire that was mailed to the home offices of 153 U.S. firms with manufacturing subsidiaries in Brazil to determine and analyze the methods used by these corporations in accounting for price-level and exchange-rate changes.

Radebaugh, Lee H. "The International Dimension of the Financial Accounting Standards Board: Translation and Disclosure of Foreign Operations." The International Journal of Accounting Education and Research, 10 (Fall 1974), 55-70.
This paper focuses on the translation of foreign currency amounts into the parent currency for consolidation with domestic operations, and on the disclosure of translation-related information.

Reckers, Philip M.J., and Martin E. Taylor. "FASB No. 8--Does It Distort Financial Statements?" The CPA Journal, 48 (August 1978), 31-34.
This article examines some of the alleged distortions created by Financial Accounting Standard No. 8 and points out how the provisions of the Statement may be inequitable and not representative of economic reality.

Rickard, D.R. "Currency Translation." The Australian Accountant, 50 (January/February 1980), 10-11.
The author discusses his feelings that translation should be at current rates, and should be combined with some form of inflation accounting.

Rodriguez, Rita M. "FASB No. 8: What Has It Done To Us?" Financial Analysts Journal, 33 (March/April 1977), 40-47.
The author examines the impact of FASB No. 8 on the reported earnings for 1974 and 1975 of 70 U.S. MNCs with large foreign direct investments in Europe, Japan and Canada.

Rogalski, Richard J., and Joseph D. Vinso. "Price Level Variations As Predictors of Flexible Exchange Rates." Journal of International Business Studies, 8 (Spring/Summer 1977), 71-82.
This study investigates the relationship between relative price levels and exchange rates with the view of establishing the validity of the purchasing power parity theory.

Rosenfield, Paul. "Accounting For Foreign Branches and Subsidiaries." The International Journal of Accounting Education and Research, 7 (Spring 1972), 35-44.
This article discusses the conceptual issues related to

translation and restatement.

Schmitz, Wolfgang. "Bretton Woods: What Changes?" Columbia Journal of World Business, 7 (January-February 1972), 13-19.
The author believes that there must be a flexibly moving system of exchange rates if world business and banking are to operate in an effective way.

Scott, David A., and Bryan C. Walker. "Foreign Currency Translation in Canada and the US." CA Magazine, 110 (November 1977), 48-53.
The authors compare the exposure draft issued by the Accounting Research Committee of the Canadian Institute of Chartered Accountants issued in June 1977 with Statement No. 8 of the Financial Accounting Standards Board in the US.

Scott, George M. "Currency Exchange Rates and Accounting Translation: A Mis-marriage?" Abacus, 11 (June 1975), 58-70.
The objective of this paper is to demonstrate that currency exchange rates are not suitable for use as an accounting translation mechanism in most circumstances. The author suggests using purchasing power parity indices as an alternative method for accounting translation.

Seidler, Lee J. "An Income Approach to the Translation of Foreign Currency Financial Statements." The CPA Journal, 42 (January 1972), 26-35.
The author proposes an income approach to the translation of foreign currency transactions and financial statements.

Shank, John K. "How Good Is FASB Statement No. 8?" Financial Analysts Journal, 32 (July/August 1976), 55-61.
This article summarizes and illustrates the main features of the new statement and discusses its implications for reporting by American-based multinationals.

Shank, John K., and Gary S. Shamis. "Reporting Foreign Currency Adjustments: A Disclosure Perspective." The Journal of Accountancy, 147 (April 1979), 59-67.
The authors point out some major problems MNCs are having with foreign currency accounting. Their proposed suggestions for improvement include highlighting the economic significance of the foreign exchange adjustment by breaking it down into types of adjustments.

Shank, John K., Jesse F. Dillard, and Richard J. Murdock. "FASB No. 8 and the Decision-Makers." Financial Executive,

48 (February 1980), 18-23.
This study, a two-phase empirical investigation, presents
specific evidence regarding the influence of Statement No.
8 on two groups whose behavioral reactions are heavily
interdependent: corporate financial managers, and investors in common equity securities who "make the market."

Shwayder, Keith R. "Accounting For Exchange Rate Fluctuations." The Accounting Review, 47 (October 1972), 747-760.
A set of rules for accounting for and measuring exposure to
currency exchange rate fluctuations is recommended. Accounting for external reporting is emphasized although much of
the discussion is also relevant for managerial accounting.

Sibley, Angus. "Exchange Control: The Cage Opens." The
Accountant's Magazine, 83 (December 1979), 509-512.
The abolition of virtually all exchange controls has far-
reaching implications for the British investor.

Smith, Alan F. "Temporal Method: Temporary Mode?"
Management Accounting, 59 (February 1978), 21-26.
This article considers the relative merits of alternative
translation methods when devaluation and revaluation occur.

Stanley, Marjorie, and Stanley B. Block. "Response By
United States Financial Managers to Financial Accounting
Standard No. 8." Journal of International Business Studies,
9 (Fall 1978), 89-99.
This study reports the response of 103 financial managers
of United States multinational corporations to the FASB
Statement No. 8 with regard to foreign currency translation.

Stanley, Marjorie T., and Stanley B. Block. "Accounting
and Economic Aspects of SFAS No. 8." The International
Journal of Accounting Education and Research, 14 (Spring
1979), 135-155.
This article presents results from a study in which the
opinions of the chief financial officers of 103 leading
MNCs were measured with regard to SFAS No. 8's impact on
earnings and valuation and its internal economic consequences. Then the economic impact of the treatment by SFAS
No. 8 of inventory and long-term debt is appraised.

Steinle, Kurt. "Currency Translation--A German View."
Accountancy, 87 (March 1976), 42-45.
The author outlines his views on the translation of foreign
currencies in world-wide consolidated financial statements.
This article is an abridged version of an article which ap-
peared in the German economic journal, Der Betrieb.

Stern, Michael. "When to Discount Your Bills of Exchange."
Accountancy, 88 (October 1977), 60-64.
This article explains the nature of bills of exchange, and
demonstrates in depth how they can be used with considerable
effect.

Teck, Alan. "Beyond FAS No. 8: Defining Other Exposures."
Management Accounting, 60 (December 1978), 54-57.
The author points out that FASB's controversial standard
created translation and transaction problems for MNCs. To
prevent wide fluctuations in foreign gains and losses, MNCs
must place more emphasis on forecasting and planning.

Teck, Alan. "International Business Under Floating Rates."
Columbia Journal of World Business, 11 (Fall 1976), 60-71.
The author examines the impact of international currency
movements on the exchange management activities of MNCs.
His discussion focuses on developments in fixed floating
rates. Corporate progress and adjustments in exposure and
international cash management practices are evaluated.

Willey, Russell W. "Foreign Currency Translation on the
Shelf." CA Magazine, 112 (April 1979), 26-31.
The author presents a critical assessment of foreign cur-
rency translation recommendations made in Canada and the
US. Problem areas are examined, and a few important as-
pects of managing foreign exchange are discussed.

Willey, Russell W. "In Defense of FAS No. 8." Management
Accounting, 61 (December 1979), 36-40.
This article summarizes the criticisms leveled against
FAS No. 8. It also lists various suggested remedies,
evaluates the criticisms, and suggests remedies for them.

Wyman, Harold E. "Analysis of Gains or Losses from Foreign
Monetary Items: An Application of Purchasing Power Parity
Concepts." The Accounting Review, 51 (July 1976), 545-558.
This paper proposes a multiequation system for analyzing
gains and losses from holding foreign monetary items, including currency, based on a concept called Purchasing Power Parity.

Accounting For Inflation In
Various Countries

Backer, Morton. "Valuation Reporting in the Netherlands:
A Real Life Example." Financial Executive, 41 (January
1973), 40-51.

This article is adapted from Professor Backer's study for the Financial Executive Research Foundation on fair value accounting.

Baden, E.J. "The Sandilands Report." The Accountant's Magazine, 79 (October 1975), 341–343.
Some aspects of the Sandilands Report are highlighted.

Baxter, W.T. "Inflation Accounting--Raising the British Standard." CA Magazine, 110 (February 1977), 36–38.
This article presents a critical look at how the Morpeth Committee would put Sandilands' theory into practice.

Baxter, W.T. "The Hyde Guide: Inflation Accounting in Britain." CA Magazine, 111 (March 1978), 53–54.
The author explains the recommendations made in the Hyde Report of November 4, 1977. This report concentrates on the correction of income in three areas: depreciation; cost of sales; and loss or gain on monetary items.

Beresford, Dennis R., and John R. Klein. "Inflation Accounting in the US and UK--a Comparison." The Journal of Accountancy, 148 (August 1979), 74–78.
The authors analyze the United States and the United Kingdom proposals for inflation accounting.

Bourn, Michael, Peter Stoney, and Robert Wynn. "Sandilands Capital Expenditure Indices--How Useful?" Accountancy, 87 (December 1976), 40–42.
The authors assess how informative these index number for capital expenditure are and whether they could be replaced by a single index without serious loss of precision.

Branch, Ben. "Common Stock Performance and Inflation: An International Comparison." The Journal of Business, 47 (January 1974), 48–52.
The author considers international data to determine to what extent, if at all, stocks may be a partial hedge against inflation.

Brennan, W. John. "Accounting for Changing Prices." The Accountant, 176 (28 April 1977), 467–469.
Efforts achieved in the UK, the US, Australia, New Zealand and Germany related to inflation accounting are summarized.

Briston, Richard J. "Sandilands: A Defence." The Accountant's Magazine, 80 (January 1976), 13–15.
The author explains why he supports the Sandilands Report on inflation accounting.

Buckley, Adrian. "Inflation Accounting: Myddleton v Sandilands--a Ringside View." Accountancy, 87 (April 1976), 60-62.
Proposals advocated by Sandilands and Myddleton for accounting for inflation are examined. The author believes the Sandilands approach is more relevant to the needs of users and should be wholeheartedly supported.

Buckley, Adrian. "Son of Sandilands--Exposure Draft 18." Accountancy, 88 (March 1977), 60-63.
The author contributes a personal view on the content and implications of ED 18. Admitting that the days of historic cost accounting should be numbered, he fears that its replacement in the time prescribed by the Inflation Accounting Steering Group with an untested system of accounting can only be a mistake.

Buckley, Adrian. "The Curate's Egg of ED 24." The Accountant, 181 (6 December 1979), 810-811.
The theme of this commentary is that ED 24 represents an unacceptable, logically dubious, accounting expedient. The author feels the incorporation of a gearing adjustment is a contrivance in direct opposition to rational accounting.

Burgert, R. "Reservations About 'Replacement Value' Accounting in the Netherlands." Abacus, 8 (December 1972), 111-126.
In this article the author sets forth briefly the theory of replacement value as devised by Professor Th. Limperg, his theory of income measurement, and the main points of criticism to his work.

Chambers, R.J. "Accounting for Inflation--Part or Whole?" The Accountant's Magazine, 80 (March 1976), 86-89.
The author explains why he feels the recommendations on accounting for inflation made by the Sandilands Report do not solve the problem.

Chambers, R.J. "Current Cost Accounting Does Not Add Up." The Australian Accountant, 46 (September 1976), 490-496.
Various aspects of the Sandilands Report are criticized.

Choi, Frederick D.S. "Foreign Inflation and Management Decisions." Management Accounting, 58 (June 1977), 21-27.
Inflation and currency translation are two problems facing most MNCs. The author proposes a method of consolidation accounting which gives the company a better command over the resources it employs in daily business operations.

Clark, Richard S. "Canada's Current Cost Accounting Pro-
posal--A Preparer's Perspective." CA Magazine, 113 (December 1980), 34-39.
The author suggests that adopting the proposals of the
Canadian Institute of Chartered Accountants' exposure draft
could be the first step in introducing a new and more relevant accounting model to many organizations, but there are
some problems.

Clarke, F.L. "Australia's Current Cost Accounting: A
Touch of This and a Dash of That." The Accountant, 176
(7 February 1977), 190-192.
Although Australia's CCA has some of the features of Sandilands' proposals, it also has some unique characteristics.
The author points out, however, that the conceptual framework it asserts is without foundation in current theories
of economics and finance.

Comer, Robert W. "Brazilian Price-Level Accounting." Management Accounting, 57 (October 1975), 41-42, 46.
This article provides a brief outline of the price-level
accounting techniques used by the Brazilians with the hope
that it will provide some insight into the economic considerations underlying inflation accounting.

Coombes, R.J., and P.H. Eddey. "Reactions of Company Accountants to CCA." The Chartered Accountant in Australia,
48 (November 1977), 40-48.
This article reports the results of a survey undertaken in
May 1977 which was directed toward company accountants, a
group much affected by the proposed introduction of the
new CCA system.

Davey, Nigel. "Overseas Subsidiaries and the CCAB Statement." Accountancy, 87 (August 1976), 68-71.
This article deals with the question of whether or not
accounts should contain a supplementary statement explaining the effects of inflation on the purchasing power of
shareholders' equity.

Denza, John. "The Calamity of Sandilands." The Accountant, 178 (13 April 1978), 490-491.
This article is the substance of a memorandum submitted
earlier in the year to the Accounting Standards Committee.
The author strongly criticizes current cost accounting, and
advises using current purchasing power accounting.

Devoe, Raymond F., Jr. "Under the Southern Cross: The
Role of Monetary Adjustment in Brazil's Economic Miracle."

<u>Financial Analysts Journal</u>, 30 (September/October 1974),
32-41, 87.
The author describes Brazil's experience with inflation and
the indexing system that the Brazilian government has developed to cope with this problem.

Dewhurst, James. "Financial and Political Consequences of
Sandilands." <u>The Accountant</u>, 175 (15 July 1976), 61-63.
The author provides a discussion on the historical facts
which led to the recommendations by the Sandilands Committee, and some views on its future.

Drury, James, and Philip Bougen. "UK Gearing Levels: An
Investigation." <u>Accountancy</u>, 91 (July 1980), 103-106.
This article is the result of an empirical study of approximately 700 UK companies made as regards gearing levels in
the UK for 1977. The study tested whether profitability,
industry, size, and sales environment had any impact on the
gearing level of a company.

Edey, Harold C. "Sandilands and the Logic of Current Cost."
<u>Accounting and Business Research</u>, 9 (Summer 1979), 191-200.
This article analyzes and criticizes the Sandilands Report's
logic.

Edwards, James Don, and John B. Barrack. "Objectives of
Financial Statements and Inflation Accounting: A Comparison of Recent British and American Proposals." <u>The International Journal of Accounting Education and Research</u>, 11
(Spring 1976), 11-32.
Recommendations of the Sandilands Committee are contrasted
with those of the Trueblood Study Group. The natures of
the two reports differ in that the Trueblood Report contains broad guidelines on what financial statements should
seek to accomplish, and the Sandilands Report contains guidance designed to alleviate a serious problem, accounting
for effects of inflation.

Edwards, J.R. "Inflation Accounting: The Best of Both
Worlds." <u>The Accountant</u>, 174 (15 January 1976), 67-68.
This article examines the basic objectives of the two
methods of inflation accounting (CCA and CPA) presently
attracting attention to provide some clue to whether there
is any scope for regarding them as complementary to one
another, rather than in direct competition.

Falk, Haim. "Current Value Accounting Preferences: The
Case For Canada." <u>The International Journal of Accounting
Education and Research</u>, 14 (Spring 1979), 29-46.

This paper reports on current value accounting preferences of Canadian financial analysts, branch managers in chartered banks, and chartered accountants who were associated with chartered accounting firms in Canada.

Fielding, John. "The Gearing Adjustment--What Is the Best Method?" Accountancy, 90 (May 1979), 73-76.
This article summarizes some the main methods which have been proposed for measuring the gearing adjustment, analyzes their strengths and weaknesses, and makes suggestions as to a preferred method.

Fisher, John. "Current Cost Accounting 1: Some Basic Problems." The Accountant, 174 (6 May 1976), 528-530.
This is the first of a two-part article. The author discusses current cost accounting recommended by the Sandilands Committee as a means of accounting for inflation.

Fisher, John. "Current Cost Accounting 2: Field Testing." The Accountant, 174 (13 May 1976), 556-558.
This is the second of a two-part article, and involves an application of the recommendations of the Sandilands report to the financial statements of five manufacturing companies. The study tests the practicability of the recommendations at a basic level to ascertain possible benefits to be derived from application, together with any related costs.

Fisher, J. "Replacement Cost Accounting--American Style." The Accountant, 176 (30 June 1977), 747-751.
The author cites the case of the US as an example of how other countries are dealing with inflation accounting.

Fleming, Robert. "Accounting for Inflation in Brazil." The Accountant's Magazine, 78 (February 1974), 58-60.
The author describes how Brazil has adjusted to inflation, and focuses on the accounting system.

Fleming, Robert. "Accounting For Inflation In Brazil." CA Magazine, 104 (April 1974), 37-41.
The author explains how a country with virtually no highly trained accountants and no sophisticated accounting bodies has managed to work out a viable system for operating price-level accounting as well as adjusting to inflation.

Fleming, Robert. "New Concepts in Brazilian Accounting for Inflation." The Accountant's Magazine, 83 (April 1979), 162-165.
In this article the author describes how a new Brazilian corporations act and new income tax regulations have af-

fected some basic concepts of accounting for inflation.

Flink, Solomon J., Assa Birati, and Meyer Ungar. "The Impact of Inflation on the Profits of Listed Firms in Israel." Accounting and Business Research, 8 (Autumn 1978), 253-257. Using the financial data of Israeli industrial corporations, this paper examines some of the effects of using nominal money figures as yardsticks for the measurement of the profitability of business entities.

Frey, Karen M. "Survey of Price-Level Accounting in Practice." The CPA Journal, 45 (May 1975), 29-34. The author discusses price-level accounting practices in countries most affected by inflation and current attention being given to the problem in other countries.

Gibbs, Martin, Keith Percy, and Richard Saville. "Sandilands--The Effect on Dividends." Accountancy, 87 (August 1976), 62-66. The authors believe that the Sandilands system should be modified by basing the cost of sales adjustment on working capital, rather than stocks, and by showing the debt-financed proportion of the holding gains as available for distribution.

Gibbs, Martin. "The Hyde Gearing Adjustment." Accountancy, 89 (February 1978), 87-89. The Hyde guidelines on inflation accounting require companies to calculate a gearing adjustment for the supplementary, inflation-adjusted statement. The author explains how to calculate the adjustment, offering solutions to problems.

Gill, Charles W., and S. Thomas Moser. "Inflation Accounting at the Crossroads." The Journal of Accountancy, 147 (January 1979), 70-78. The authors offer a global survey of where inflation accounting stands and where it is going. This article was originally published in the Summer 1978 issue of World (Peat, Marwick, Mitchell & Co.).

Goch, Desmond. "Current Value Accounting: Canada's Contribution." The Accountant, 176 (24 February 1977), 218-219. The author outlines the Canadian contribution toward solving the problem of accounting for inflation.

Grinyer, John. "Sandilands: From the Frying-Pan Into The Fire." Accountancy, 87 (January 1976), 34-41.

The Sandilands' CCA system and the profit concepts underlying it are outlined. The author thinks that both replacement cost operating profits and current purchasing
power accounts should be provided.

Hauworth, William P., II. "A Comparison of Various International Proposals on Inflation Accounting: A Practitioner's View." The International Journal of Accounting
Education and Research, 16 (Fall 1980), 63-82.
This paper summarizes and compares the methods to give an
accounting recognition to the effects of changing prices
that are now required or have been proposed in a number of
countries throughout the world.

Houston, A.W. "Boardroom View of Sandilands." The Accountant, 175 (26 August 1976), 243-244.
The Sandilands Report highlighted the damage inflicted upon
companies by political attitudes toward inflation. This
article sets out some ideas on salvage measures.

Johnston, Trevor. "Current Cost Accounting in New Zealand."
The Accountant's Magazine, 83 (February 1979), 73-74.
New Zealand's experiences with inflation and inflation accounting are very similar to those of the UK. The latest
development there is the issue of "CCA Guidelines" which
call for both a supplementary profit and loss account and
a supplementary balance sheet.

Kenley, W.J. "Accounting Under Conditions of Inflation:
Important Developments in New Zealand." The Australian
Accountant, 46 (June 1976), 280-285.
The author describes a project, a large-scale empirical
test of the major methods of accounting under conditions of
inflation, being undertaken by the Department of Management
Studies at the University of Waikato, New Zealand.

Kennedy, Charles. "Fixed Assets and the Hyde Gearing Adjustment." Journal of Business Finance & Accounting, 5
(Winter 1978), 393-406.
In this article the author compares and differentiates between the Godley-Cripps' and Hyde's proposals for gearing
adjustment to current cost accounts.

Lafferty, Michael. "International Moves in Inflation Accounting." The Accountant, 176 (27 January 1977), 104-106.
The author surveys moves in inflation accounting in countries and organizations which appear to have most direct
significance for British-based companies.

Lay, David W. "CCA--Canada's Proposed Solution to Inflation Accounting." CA Magazine, 113 (February 1980), 44-48.
This article compares FASB No. 33 in the USA with the Canadian Accounting Research Committee Proposal. The author points out that in spite of the similarities there are some disturbing differences between them.

Leech, Stewart A., and Denis J. Pratt. "Current Cost Accounting in Australia, New Zealand, and the United Kingdom: A Comparative Study." The International Journal of Accounting Education and Research, 13 (Spring 1978), 105-118.
This paper investigates the evolution of CCA in Australia, examines the Australian CCA standard, and compares it with the UK and New Zealand proposals.

Leech, Stewart A., Denis J. Pratt, and W.G.W. Magill. "Company Asset Revaluations and Inflation in Australia, 1950-1975." Journal of Business Finance & Accounting, 5 (Winter 1978), 353-362.
The objectives of this article are to examine the incidence of asset revaluations made by companies listed on the Melbourne Stock Exchange from 1950 to 1975; to assess the effect of revaluations on companies' rates of return and total assets; and to test the hypothesis that a positive and significant relationship exists between company asset revaluations and various measures of inflation.

Lemke, Kenneth W. "The Achilles Heel of Sandilands." CA Magazine, 109 (September 1976), 37-41.
The author claims that by failing to consider technological change, the Sandilands systems of current cost accounting can result in seriously misleading financial statements.

Lorensen, Leonard, and Paul Rosenfield. "Management Information and Foreign Inflation." The Journal of Accountancy, 138 (December 1974), 98-102.
The authors discuss whether managers of foreign subsidiaries should use financial statements that have been restated for general price level changes in the foreign countries.

Marriott, Russell G. "CCA: A Comparison of the Australian and UK Proposals." The Australian Accountant, 49 (October 1979), 612-617.
This article evaluates how Australia's CCA proposals compare with those of the UK contained in Exposure Draft 24, "Current Cost Accounting," and accompanying Guidance Notes.

Mattessich, Richard V. "The Canadian CCA Exposure Draft--A Flawed Approach." CA Magazine, 113 (November 1980), 48-51.

The author examines and critiques the CCICA's 1979 Exposure Draft issued by the Accounting Research Committee, stating that neither the UK Standard nor the Canadian Exposure Draft have tried to aid the reader's understanding.

McCosh, Andrew M. "Implications of Sandilands for Non-UK Accountants." The Journal of Accountancy, 141 (March 1976), 42-50.
England's inflationary ills are examined. The author stresses the Sandilands report and examines the implications of its proposal for both the UK and other countries which might adopt similar roles.

McCosh, Andrew M., and Richard F. Vancil. "Reconciling Sandilands with Current Purchasing Power Adjustments." Accounting and Business Research, 6 (Summer 1976), 162-170.
This article tries to reconcile the replacement cost approach taken by Sandilands to adjustments for general price level.

McKinnon, James. "Perspectives on the Hyde Guidelines." The Accountant's Magazine, 81 (December 1977), 497-499.
This article provides a review of the interim recommendations on inflation accounting, published in November 1977 by the Accounting Standards Committee.

Merrett, A.J., and Allen Sykes. "What Sandilands DIDN'T Say." Accountancy, 86 (November 1975), 42-47.
The authors call for a major effort directed towards clarifying the theoretical and empirical case for establishing the profitability of British industry, and then define the "norms" of profitability on the Sandilands basis to which government and industry must strive.

Mitchell, G.B. "Current Cost Accounting: Canadian and New Zealand Contributions." The Australian Accountant, 46 (December 1976), 677-679.
The author outlines Canadian and New Zealand releases on current cost (or value) accounting, and predicts that in the 1980s there will be a generally uniform approach to CCA in the major English speaking countries.

Moir, John A.W. "Inflation Accounting for Companies: In Support of PSSAP 7." The Accountant's Magazine, 78 (November 1974), 433-436.
The author strongly favors the Provisional Statement of Standard Accounting Practice No. 7, "Accounting for Changes in the Purchasing Power of Money," and this article illustrates his thinking on the problem.

Morpeth, D.S. "Practical Problems of Inflation Accounting."
The Accountant, 174 (8 April 1976), 416-418.
This paper, presented to a conference of UK government accountants, is concerned with the problems of transforming
the Sandilands proposals into a practical system of accounting for inflation.

Muis, Jules W. "Current Value Accounting in the Netherlands: Fact or Fiction?" The Accountant's Magazine, 79
(November 1975), 377-379.
The author summarizes the developments related to current
value accounting in the Netherlands both by writers and in
the accounting practice.

Muis, Jules W. "The Hofstra Report--Inflation Accounting
For Tax Purposes." The Accountant's Magazine, 82 (May
1978), 207-208.
This article summarizes and analyzes a report prepared by
the Dutch professor to the Dutch government to investigate
the desirability and practicability of a revision of the
Dutch taxation system aimed at neutralizing the distorting
effects of inflation.

Mumford, Michael J. "Indices and the Hyde Gearing Adjustment." The Accountant's Magazine, 82 (October 1978), 422-
423.
This article criticizes the Hyde gearing adjustment for in-
corporating two incompatible alternative treatments of net
monetary assets and liabilities. A reconciliation between
the two is demonstrated, and a simpler version recommended.

Myddelton, D.R. "Inflation Accounting and the Unreal World
of Sandilands." Accountancy, 87 (February 1976), 34-37.
The author concludes that the Sandilands report reveals a
totally unrealistic view and fails to deal with inflation.
In contrast, CPP, in the author's opinion, represents a
comprehensive system for adjusting accounts to allow for
monetary inflation.

Peasnell, K.V., and L.C.L. Skerratt. "How Well Does a Single Index Represent the Nineteen Sandilands Plant and Machinery Indices?" Journal of Accounting Research, 15
(Spring 1977), 108-119.
This paper presents some empirical evidence concerning the
commonality among the set of nineteen official government
price indices of capital expenditure on plant and machinery
which Sandilands put forward for the partial implementation
of CCA. The question it attempts to answer is: What information is provided by these detailed indices, as compared

41

with a total plant and machinery index?

Perrin, J.R. "Current Cost Accounting--A Reply to Professor Chambers." The Australian Accountant, 46 (December
1976), 680-684.
The author defends Current Cost Accounting and the Sandilands Report, in response to criticisms made in an article
(The Australian Accountant, September 1976), by Professor
R.J. Chambers.

Platt, Arthur. "The Dividend Distribution--Where Sandilands Fails." Accountancy, 87 (July 1976), 70-74.
The author examines the CCA recommendations and finds that
if profits calculated as advocated by the Sandilands Report
are distributed in full, then this will lead to what is in
effect a payment out of capital.

Platt, W.H. "Analysis of Aspects of the Treatment of Monetary Gains and Losses in the Hyde Guidelines and ED 24."
Journal of Business Finance & Accounting, 6 (Winter 1979),
579-601.
This paper evaluates the treatment of gains and losses on
monetary assets and liabilities in the CCA system proposed
in the Interim Recommendations on Inflation Accounting
usually referred to as the Hyde Guidelines.

Rayburn, Frank, and Barney Cargile. "SSAP 16 and SFAS 33:
Different Approaches to Accounting for Changing Prices."
The Accountant's Magazine, 85 (March 1981), 74-76.
The authors compare the proposals recently issued in the UK
and the US on how to account for changing prices.

Rayman, R.A. "An Accountant's Adventures in Sandilands."
Accountancy, 87 (August 1976), 58-60.
The author criticizes the Sandilands Report, and claims that
it rests on weak foundations.

Rosenfield, Paul. "The Golden Opportunity." Accountancy,
86 (February 1975), 37-41.
This article discusses the methods of treating foreign
operations in general purchasing statements proposed by the
standard-setting bodies of several different countries. The
author advocates the translate-restate method to avoid in-
corporating foreign inflation into statements.

Sale, J. Timothy, and Robert W. Scapens. "Accounting for
the Effects of Changing Prices." The Journal of Accountancy, 150 (July 1980), 82-87.
The authors discuss the evolution of the standard-setting

process in the UK related to accounting for changing prices, the similarities and differences between SSAP 16 and FASB Statement No. 33, and the implications for the US accounting profession of the UK experience.

Sale, J. Timothy, and Robert W. Scapens. "A Sample of Sandilands." CA Magazine, 110 (January 1977), 45-48.
This article illustrates how the Sandilands proposal of current cost system might work in practice. It also compares it with the US financial accounting standard on inflation.

Scapens, Bob. "The Treatment of Inflation Overseas." Accountancy, 87 (January 1976), 54-59.
This article reports major developments that have taken place since 1973, drawing attention to the direction of thought in several countries (other than England) where the actual or proposed accounting practices differ from those of the British practices.

Shaw, J.C. "The Hyde Gearing Adjustment." The Accountant's Magazine, 82 (March 1978), 104-106.
This article discusses some aspects of the Hyde Guidelines insofar as they relate to monetary adjustments; that is, the adjustment in the supplementary statement in respect of net monetary assets or the gearing adjustment when there are net monetary liabilities.

Shaw, J.C. "Sandilands: A Practising Accountant's View." The Accountant's Magazine, 80 (January 1976), 9-13.
The author explains why he welcomes a CCA system in the areas of taxation, auditing and reporting, and financial advising.

Stamp, Edward, and Alister K. Mason. "Current Cost Accounting: British Panacea or Quagmire?" The Journal of Accountancy, 143 (April 1977), 66-73.
The authors outline the background of the British Morpeth report, summarizing its major provisions, and appraise its effects for US accountants.

Stamp, Edward. "ED 18 and Current Cost Accounting: A Review Article." Accounting and Business Research, 7 (Spring 1977), 83-94.
This is a review article of Exposure Draft No. 18 on current cost accounting that was issued by the Accounting Standards Committee on November 30, 1976.

Standish, Peter. "Accounting Responses to Inflation in the European Economic Community." The International Journal of

Accounting Education and Research, 11 (Fall 1975), 167-186.
This paper deals with the methods of accounting for inflation by the members of the EEC.

Standish, Peter. "Inflation Accounting Down Under." Accountancy, 87 (March 1976), 48-53.
This article reports on developments in Australia related to inflation accounting, comparing them to UK developments.

Standish, Peter. "Can Auditing Survive Sandilands?" Accountancy, 87 (November 1976), 44-49.
The author believes that an inflation accounting Standard based on Sandilands will extend subjectivity in accounting, especially in valuation of non-monetary assets and estimation of associated costs.

Stevenson, K.M., and R.G. Marriott. "Current Cost Accounting." The Chartered Accountant in Australia, 50 (June 1980), 58-64.
In the wake of SSAP 16, the authors provide a comparison of the UK and Australian approaches to current cost accounting.

Stobie, Bruce. "The New South African Inflation Accounting Guideline." The Accountant's Magazine, 83 (January 1979), 26-27.
The author reviews recent South African current cost accounting recommendations made by the National Council of Chartered Accountants in South Africa in "Guideline on Disclosure of Effects of Changing Prices on Financial Results."

Taylor, Dennis. "An Inflation Accounting Research Project in New Zealand." The Accountant's Magazine, 85 (October 1981), 347-349.
This article provides an up-date on the University of Waikato's heavy involvement in applied research and continuing education as inflation accounting moves closer to the stage of full CCA adoption in New Zealand.

Trow, Donald G. "The New Zealand Approach to Inflation Accounting." The Accountant's Magazine, 81 (February 1977), 65.
The author discusses the report of the New Zealand Government Committee of Inquiry into Inflation Accounting which was released on December 9, 1976.

Tweedie, David P. "Current Cost Accounting: UK Controversies and Overseas 'Solutions.'" The Accountant's Magazine, 81 (August 1977), 343-348.
In light of the controversy surrounding the future of CCA

in the UK, this article looks at the lessons to be learned from the ways in which three Commonwealth countries have tackled the main area of contention raised by ED 18.

Tweedie, D.P. "The Hyde Guidelines--How Are They To Be Interpreted?" The Accountant's Magazine, 82 (April 1978), 149-152.
This article considers the meaning of the Hyde Guidelines by studying, in turn, the implications of each of its three proposed adjustments.

Van Seventer, A. "Replacement Value Theory in Modern Dutch Accounting." The International Journal of Accounting Education and Research, 11 (Fall 1975), 67-94.
The author provides a discussion of some fundamental principles of the replacement value theory in the Netherlands.

Volten, Henk. "A Response From the Netherlands." The Journal of Accountancy, 145 (March 1978), 44-45.
In their article in the April 1977 issue of The Journal of Accountancy, E. Stamp and A. Mason refer to the failure of the Dutch to issue any official pronouncements on requiring the use of current value accounting. In this article, the author discusses the progress of accounting pronouncements in the Netherlands. A reply from Stamp and Mason follows.

Westwick, Chris. "Inflation Accounting: Sandilands, PSSAP 7, But What Now?" Accountancy, 86 (December 1975), 38-39.
The author argues that what is really required is not CCA as advocated by Sandilands, nor CPP as would have been required if provisional SSAP 7 had been adopted as a full standard, but a combination of CCA and CPP.

Westwick, Chris. "How Did the Steering Group Tackle the Problems of CCA?" Accountancy, 88 (January 1977), 42-44.
The author examines some of the problems which the Inflation Accounting Steering Group tackled during the preparation of the Exposure Draft on current cost accounting (ED 18), and, where appropriate, compares proposals with those of SSAP 7 and Sandilands.

Westwick, C.A. "ED 24's Gearing Adjustment--Some Queries and Proposals." The Accountant, 181 (16 August 1979), 232-233.
The author argues that the ED 24 gearing adjustment led to a profit being attributable to shareholders but which could not be distributed to them unless borrowing was increased, or the business was run down, or surplus cash used from

previous years.

Westwick, C.A. "ED 24's Gearing Adjustment: Some Queries and Proposals (2)." The Accountant, 181 (23 August 1979), 260-262.
In the conclusion of a two-part article on the problems and consequences associated with the capital maintenance concept implied by ED 24's gearing adjustment, the author demonstrates his argument by numerical example.

Westwick, C.A. "The Lessons to be Learned from the Development of Inflation Accounting in the UK." Accounting and Business Research, 10 (Autumn 1980), 353-373.
The purpose of this paper is to recount the story of the development of inflation accounting in the UK from 1946 to 1980, then to see what lessons can be learned from it.

Winfield, Ray R. "Accounting for Inflation--A New Zealand Project." The Accountant's Magazine, 83 (July 1979), 283-284.
In New Zealand, academic and practising accountants are co-operating closely in a project to field test and implement a system of price-level accounting. This article explains how the project was set up and how it is coping.

Wollstadt, Roger D. "The Challenge of the Sandilands Report." Management Accounting, 57 (July 1976), 15-22.
The author sets out the major conclusions of the Sandilands Report, with some of the philosophy and reasoning behind those conclusions.

Woo, John C.H. "Accounting for Inflation: Some International Models." Management Accounting, 59 (February 1978), 37-43.
This is a comparative analysis of financial statements reflecting the methods used in the UK, the Netherlands, and Brazil, as compared to the historical method used in the US relative to accounting for inflation.

Zeff, Stephen, and Ovando Hugo. "Inflation Accounting and the Development of Accounting Principles in Chile." The Accountant's Magazine, 79 (June 1975), 212-214.
Chile has the highest rate of inflation in the world, and yet has "the biggest middle class and least poverty in South America." The authors describe how the accounting profession in Chile is coping with such a situation.

Financial Disclosure in
Various Countries

Adelberg, Arthur Harris. "Forecasting the the US Dilemma."
Accountancy, 87 (October 1976), 83-90.
This article deals with the difficulty of including fore-
casts in annual reports, contrasting UK and US views.

Anderson, R. "The Usefulness of Accounting and Other Information Disclosed in Corporate Annual Reports to Institutional Investors in Australia." Accounting and Business
Research, 11 (Autumn 1981), 259-265.
The purpose of this paper is to report the findings of an
empirical investigation into the usefulness of annual reports to institutional investors in Australia.

Baker, H. Kent, Robert H. Chanhall, John A. Haslem, and
Rogert H. Juchau. "Disclosure of Material Information: A
Cross-National Comparison." The International Journal of
Accounting Education and Research, 13 (Fall 1977), 1-18.
This study examines the information needs of individual in-
vestors in the United States and Australia. It also iden-
tifies important sources of information used by these in-
vestors in analyzing common stock.

Barrett, M. Edgar. "Annual Report Disclosure: Are American Reports Superior?" Journal of International Business
Studies, 6 (Fall 1975), 15-24.
The author examines the extent and quality of corporate financial disclosure among the largest publicly-held corporations in seven countries during the 1963-1972 period.

Barrett, M. Edgar. "Financial Reporting Practices: Disclosure and Comprehensiveness in an International Setting."
Journal of Accounting Research, 14 (Spring 1976), 10-26.
This study focuses upon the overall extent of financial
disclosure and the degree of comprehensiveness of firms'
financial statements reflected in the annual reports of
major firms located in seven countries.

Barrett, M. Edgar. "The Extent of Disclosure in Annual Reports of Large Companies in Seven Countries." The International Journal of Accounting Education and Research, 12
(Spring 1977), 1-26.
This study examines whether or not the extent of financial
disclosure in foreign annual reports is significantly different from that found in the U.S.

Bavishi, Vinod B., and Harold E. Wyman. "Foreign Operations

Disclosure by U.S. Based Multinational Corporations: Are
They Adequate?" <u>The International Journal of Accounting
Education and Research</u>, 16 (Fall 1980), 153-168.
This paper explains what is required by the Financial
Accounting Standards Board, and contrasts the FASB require-
ments with information desired by other organizations.

Benston, George J. "Public (US) Compared to Private (UK)
Regulation of Corporate Financial Disclosure." <u>The Accounting Review</u>, 51 (July 1976), 483-498.
This paper explores the differences, costs and benefits of
the US and UK systems of regulation of corporate financial
disclosure and concludes that, in many important respects,
private (UK) regulation is preferable.

Castle, Eric F. "The Problems of Consolidation of Accounts
of a Multinational Enterprise: Shell Group of Companies--
Shell Transport and Trading Company, Limited, UK." <u>The International Journal of Accounting Education and Research</u>,
16 (Fall 1980), 209-219.
The author describes accounting problems encountered by
the Shell Group of Companies.

Chang, Lucia S., and Kenneth S. Most. "An International
Comparison of Investor Uses of Financial Statements." <u>The
International Journal of Accounting Education and Research</u>,
17 (Fall 1981), 43-60.
The objective of this research is to test the following hypothesis: financial statements published as a part of corporate annual reporting are used for investment decisions.

Choi, Frederick D.S. "Financial Disclosure and Entry to the
European Capital Market." <u>Journal of Accounting Research</u>,
11 (Autumn 1973), 159-175.
The author provides some evidence concerning the relationship between financial information and a firm's entry into
a capital market.

Choi, Frederick D.S. "Primary-Secondary Reporting: A
Cross-Cultural Analysis." <u>The International Journal of
Accounting Education and Research</u>, 16 (Fall 1980), 83-104.
This paper examines a proposed reporting framework which
recommends that multiple sets of statements, primary and
secondary, be prepared for a firm with audiences of interest in more than one country.

Dhaliwal, Dan S. "Improving the Quality of Corporate Financial Disclosure." <u>Accounting and Business Research</u>, 10
(Autumn 1980), 385-391.

An alternative approach to the problem of improving financial disclosure in annual reports is proposed.

Evans, Thomas G. "The Most and Shillinglaw Debate Updated." _Accountancy_, 86 (July 1975), 36-39.
This article is about the international comparability of accounting statements. The author concludes that the American system is superior, primarily due to the American consolidation policy and presentation of more financial statements.

Ferris, Kenneth R., and David C. Hayes. "Some Evidence On the Determinants of Profit Forecast Accuracy in the United Kingdom." _The International Journal of Accounting Education and Research_, 12 (Spring 1977), 27-36.
This study describes the methodology and result of an investigation undertaken to identify some of the determinants of profit forecast accuracy in the United Kingdom.

Firth, Michael. "A Study of the Consensus of the Perceived Importance of Disclosure of Individual Items in Corporate Annual Reports." _The International Journal of Accounting Education and Research_, 14 (Fall 1978), 57-70.
The major purpose of this study is to provide empirical evidence relating to the importance of disclosure in corporate annual reports in the United Kingdom.

Firth, Michael. "The Impact of Size, Stock Market Listing, and Auditors on Voluntary Disclosure in Corporate Annual Reports." _Accounting and Business Research_, 9 (Autumn 1979), 273-280.
The purpose of this article is to report on a study into the relationship of disclosure in corporate annual reports and three firm-specific characteristics that may, or may not, have some influence over the level of disclosure.

Gray, S.J. "Statistical Information and Extensions in European Financial Disclosure." _The International Journal of Accounting Education and Research_, 13 (Spring 1978), 27-40.
This paper considers the following question with reference to the European investment environment: Should an analysis of financial statements be provided in addition to the financial statements themselves?

Gray, S.J. "Managerial Forecasts and European Multinational Company Reporting." _Journal of International Business Studies_, 9 (Fall 1978), 21-32.
The aim of this article is to establish the extent of

disclosure of forecasts in practice and to ascertain any differences in disclosure as between companies based in the different EEC countries.

Jaggi, B.L. "The Impact of the Cultural Environment on Financial Disclosures." The International Journal of Accounting Education and Research, 10 (Spring 1975), 75-84.
This paper examines the impact of the cultural environment and individual value orientations on information disclosures. Based on this examination, hypotheses as to the reliability of financial disclosures are developed.

McKeon, Ashley. "Communication in Annual Reports." The Australian Accountant, 46 (August 1976), 420-423.
The author makes a plea for companies to include in their annual reports information designed to communicate a true and fair view of the enterprise.

Meins, Paul G. "Reporting Overseas Pension Costs." Accountancy, 88 (October 1977), 110.
The author discusses problems in reporting pension costs in overseas subsidiaries, and suggests a possible approach.

Morley, Michael F. "The Value Added Statement in Britain." The Accounting Review, 54 (July 1979), 618-629.
This article relates the structure of the Value Added Statement to the underlying theory of company team membership; the Statement is contrasted with the earnings statement which it resembles.

Mueller, Gerhard G. "An International View of Accounting and Disclosure." The International Journal of Accounting Education and Research, 8 (Fall 1972), 117-134.
This paper seeks to demonstrate that a major international trend toward increased financial disclosure has developed since the mid-1960s, and that disclosure improvements offer more hope for financial reporting during the 1970s than advances in accounting development.

Murphy, George J. "Financial Statement Disclosure and Corporate Law: The Canadian Experience." The International Journal of Accounting Education and Research, 15 (Spring 1980), 87-100.
The purpose of this paper is to chronicle the changes in legislated financial statement disclosure requirements in Canada and to indicate, where possible, the source of the influences which gave rise to those changes.

Parker, L.D. "Corporate Annual Reports: A Failure to Com-

municate." The International Journal of Accounting Education and Research, 16 (Spring 1980), 35-48.
This paper emphasizes the seriousness of the failure of the corporate annual report to communicate with the bulk of private investors, and identifies the magnitude of the problem as evidenced by empirical studies in the UK, Canada, Australia, the US and New Zealand.

Segmental Reporting

Arnold, Jerry, William W. Holder, and M. Herschel Mann. "International Reporting Aspects of Segment Disclosure." The International Journal of Accounting Education and Research, 16 (Fall 1980), 125-135.
Given that companies have discretion in defining geographic areas, it is not clear on an a priori basis what level of disaggregation exists in practice. The purpose of this paper is to investigate this question empirically.

Compagnoni, Albert, and Joel G. Siegel. "Segmental Reporting: The American Scene." The Australian Accountant, 50 (May 1980), 226-231.
Advantages and disadvantages of segmental reporting are discussed, and an outline is given of the U.S. profession's response to demands for segmented information.

Emmanuel, C.R., and S.J. Gray. "Segmental Disclosures and the Segment Identification Problem." Accounting and Business Research, 8 (Winter 1977), 37-50.
This article is the result of a study to determine whether or not information disclosed accurately reflects the business and international operations of companies concerned.

Emmanuel, C.R., and S.J. Gray. "The Presentation of Segment Reports." Accountancy, 89 (June 1978), 91-92.
The authors suggest presenting segmental information in a matrix form, mainly because it is a more comprehensive reflection of reality.

Emmanuel, C.R., and S.J. Gray. "Segmental Disclosure by Multibusiness Multinational Companies: A Proposal." Accounting and Business Research, 8 (Summer 1978), 169-177.
This paper indicates deficiencies of current segmental disclosure requirements in the UK, and refers to empirical evidence which reveals the wide variety of practices followed.

Emmanuel, C.R., and R.H. Pick. "The Predictive Ability of

UK Segment Reports." Journal of Business Finance & Accounting, 7 (Summer 1980), 201-218.
This study tests the hypothesis that industrial segment sales and profit disclosure, together with industry sales projections published in various government and economic institutional sources, provide significantly more accurate estimates of future total-entity sales and earnings than do those procedures that rely totally on consolidated data.

Ezzamel, M.A., and K. Hilton. "Divisionalisation in British Industry: A Preliminary Study." Accounting and Business Research, 10 (Spring 1980), 197-214.
This study evaluates the impact of divisionalization on one measure of the economic performance of companies.

Gray, S.J. "Segment Reporting and the EEC Multinationals." Journal of Accounting Research, 16 (Autumn 1978), 242-253.
This paper focuses on segmental reporting of multinationals in the EEC. It explores the extent to which segment reports are provided in practice, and whether or not there are differences in disclosure between companies based in different countries in the EEC.

Miller, Malcom C., and Mark R. Scott. "Segmentation of Consolidated Financial Statements." The Chartered Accountant in Australia, 50 (June 1980), 33-36.
This article is the result of an analysis done by the authors on the 1979 annual reports of 100 listed companies. Their findings regarding segmental reporting are given.

Mirza, A.M. "Australian Auditors' Views on Reporting for Segments of a Business." The Australian Accountant, 46 (March 1976), 86-90.
The results of a survey of Australian public accounting firms to learn their opinion of the proposition that diversified companies should provide detailed information on a segment basis in their published reports are presented.

Social Responsibility Disclosure In
Various Countries

Alexander, Michael O. "Social Accounting If You Please." CA Magazine, 102 (January 1973), 23-33.
This article investigates how accounting information could be developed to help the corporation communicate within its social and human dimensions--its shareholders, employees, customers, and surrounding communities.

Anderson, R.H. "Attitudes of Chartered Accountants to Social Responsibility Disclosure in Australia." The Chartered Accountant in Australia, 50 (June 1980), 13-16. The purpose of this article is to report the findings of a questionnaire survey into the attitudes of Australian chartered accountants to social reporting by companies.

Bostock, Christopher. "The Corporate Report 3: A Private View from the Private Sector." The Accountant, 174 (22 April 1976), 471-473. The author argues that there are strict limits to the extent to which a private sector entity should be asked to meet the needs of the business contact group.

Brown, Andrew. "Social (R)Evolution and the EEC." The Accountant's Magazine, 85 (March 1981), 83-84. The author examines the scope and content of an EEC proposed Directive which could mean that large national and multinational companies will be legally bound to establish employee consultation procedures.

Brownell, Peter. "Social Accounting--Go; or No Go!" The Australian Accountant, 7 (August 1977), 430-433. The author outlines problems of defining, measuring and communicating the social responsibility of corporations.

Catherwood, Sir Frederick. "Social Responsibility--the Seamless Robe." Accountancy, 85 (October 1974), 34-35. The author discusses several ways in which accountanta can contribute to social responsibility.

Chastain, Clark E. "Environmental Accounting--U.S. & U.K." Accountancy, 84 (December 1973), 10-13. The role of the accountant in pollution control in the United States and Britain is compared.

Holmes, Geoffrey. "How UK Companies Report to Their Employees." Accountancy, 88 (November 1977), 64-68. This article examines a number of employee reports to find out how companies are devising their own guidelines.

Hussey, Roger. "France Has a Social Audit." Accountancy, 89 (February 1978), 111-113. The author describes the requirement of the Social Audit in France and the background that led to it.

Jaggi, Bikki. "An Analysis of Corporate Social Reporting in Germany." The International Journal of Accounting Education and Research, 15 (Spring 1980), 35-45.

This paper analyzes Deutsche Shell's social disclosure
model. The concepts of a social accounts statement and a
value-added statement receive special scrutiny.

McComb, Desmond. "Some Guidelines on Social Accounting in
the U.S." Accountancy, 89 (April 1978), 50-52.
The author suggests that the Americans' experience could
provide accountants in the UK with some guidelines to reporting on matters which are of social concern.

Most, Kenneth. "Corporate Social Reporting in Germany."
The Accountant, 176 (10 February 1977), 164-166.
The author discusses a new kind of annual report by the
German subsidiary of the Shell Group, Deutsche Shell AG.

Parker, L.D. "Financial Reporting to Corporate Employees."
The Chartered Accountant in Australia, 47 (March 1977), 5-9.
This paper outlines the forms which the communication of
information concerning corporate financial performance by
presentations specifically designed for employees can take,
its potential and problems, and its significance for Australian business and the accounting profession.

Parker, L.D. "Accounting for Corporate Social Responsibi-
lity--The Task of Measurement." The Chartered Accountant
in Australia, 48 (October 1977), 5-15.
This paper discusses the rationale behind Social Responsibility Reporting, the categories of interested parties,
general patterns of disclosure available and the justification for developing precise measurement techniques.

Parker, L.D. "Social Accounting--Don't Wait For It." The
Accountant's Magazine, 80 (February 1976), 50-52.
Aimed at accountants both in practice and in industry, this
article explains, in practical terms, what social accounting
is, why some form of it should be tried and how an accountant might attempt to undertake it initially.

Parkes, Hugh. "Future Prospects in Accounting for Social
Responsibility by Australian Firms." The Australian Accountant, 51 (May 1981), 246-248.
A list is presented which highlights areas to which social
responsibility coverage could be extended if a company considered it to be desirable.

Reichmann, Thomas, and Christoph Lange. "The Value Added
Statement As Part of Corporate Social Reporting." Manage-
ment International Review, 21 (1981/4), 17-22.
The purpose of this paper is to discuss the aims of the

Value Added Statement as part of corporate social reporting to enable conclusions to be drawn as to the suitable format to meet these aims.

Robertson, John. "Corporate Social Reporting By New Zealand Companies." Journal of Contemporary Business, 7 (Winter 1978), 113-133.
This paper reports the findings of a survey undertaken to assess the extent and kind of corporate social reporting in New Zealand company annual reports.

Schreuder, Hein. "Employees and the Corporate Social Report: The Dutch Case." The Accounting Review, 56 (April 1981), 294-308.
This paper presents the results of a research project carried out to probe reactions of employees toward social reports actually published in the Netherlands.

Sherwood, Kenneth A. "The Corporate Report 2: Will New-Style Reports be Indigestible?" The Accountant, 174 (8 April 1976), 419-421.
This article is a critique of the discussion paper, "The Corporate Report." It is concerned with providing additional or alternative information in corporate reports.

Tweedie, D.P. "The Corporate Report: Evolution or Revolution." The Accountant's Magazine, 79 (October 1975), 343-346.
This article considers the rationale for extending the scope of annual financial reports to meet the needs of a wider user group and also to examine the findings of recent empirical research.

Van Den Bergh, Richard. "Time to Speed Corporate Social Accounting." Accountancy, 87 (April 1976), 50-53.
The author discusses the accountant's role in the development of social accounting and social auditing.

Wells, Louis T. "Social Cost/Benefit Analysis for MNCs." Harvard Business Review, 53 (March-April 1975), 40-50.
The author surveys the techniques of social analysis and points out how the social cost/benefit approach can also provide a framework for sensible price setting and intelligent resource allocation at home.

Wright, M.G. "The Corporate Report 4: Extended Information May be Counter-productive." The Accountant, 174 (27 May 1976), 619-620.
The author gives his views on "The Corporate Report."

Amernic, Joel H., and Nissim Aranya. "Public Accountants'
Independence: Some Evidence In A Canadian Context." The
International Journal of Accounting Education and Research,
16 (Spring 1981), 11-34.
This paper reviews the literature to discover insights into
the topic which might be helpful in formulating research
questions. It also reports the results of a survey of Canadian CAs' opinion related to independence.

Anderson, J.V.R. "'True and Fair' in the EEC." The Accountant, 174 (4 March 1976), 284-286.
This article discusses the concept of "true and fair" in the
context of corporate reporting, as background to the likely
impact of the revised Fourth Directive of the EEC.

Barlev, Benzion. "The Initial Selection of Independent
Public Accountants: An Empirical Investigation." The International Journal of Accounting Education and Research,
12 (Spring 1977), 37-52.
This study empirically investigates the process of selecting
a public accountant in newly formed, medium sized, privately
owned Israeli industrial companies.

Bartholomew, E.G. "The EEC and Auditors' Qualifications."
The Accountant's Magazine, 82 (August 1978), 33-35.
This article outlines the main proposals and highlights some
problematical areas in the EEC's draft Eighth Directive on
auditors' qualifications and its impact on UK accountants.

Briner, Ernst K. "New Horizons For Internal Auditing in
Europe." The Internal Auditor, 32 (September/October 1975),
58-64.
This article presents a brief summary of a seminar on external and internal auditing held in Switzerland.

Briston, Richard J. "The Changing Role of Government Audit
in Developing Countries: Implications for UK Accounting
Firms." The Accountant's Magazine, 83 (August 1979), 325-
327.
This article describes what some African States are aspiring
to in the area of government audits departments and what
Egypt has already achieved, and warns that such trends have
far-reaching implications for the international work of UK
firms of accountants.

Court, Peter. "The Multinational Audit Team: Who Holds
the Reins?" Accountancy, 91 (October 1980), 85-88.

The co-ordination implications of a multinational audit engagement are examined.

Crum, William F. "The European Public Accountant." <u>Management Accounting</u>, 56 (March 1975), 41-44, 54-55.
The author explores the process of educating and training individuals preparing for a career in public accounting in several European countries to find out how it differs from that of their counterparts in the US.

Davidson, A.G. "Current Events Affecting Auditors in the United States and Canada: Possible Relevance to Australia." <u>The Chartered Accountant in Australia</u>, 49 (August 1978), 19-24.
This article summarizes the Metcalf and Cohen Reports in the US and the Adams Report in Canada, and assesses their relevance to the Australian scene.

Dykxhoorn, Hans, and Kathleen E. Sinning. "Wirtschaft-sprüfer Perception and Auditor Independence." <u>The Accounting Review</u>, 56 (January 1981), 97-107.
This paper discusses the results of a survey conducted to ascertain the perceptions of Wirtschaftsprüfer (German auditors) concerning auditors' independence.

Dykxhoorn, Hans J., and Kathleen E. Sinning. "The Independence Issue Concerning German Auditors: A Synthesis." <u>The International Journal of Accounting Education and Research</u>, 16 (Spring 1981), 163-182.
This paper deals with the issue of independence affecting German auditors by reviewing and discussing the relevant German literature and independence regulations.

Fantl, Irving L. "Control and the Internal Audit in the Multinational Firm." <u>The International Journal of Accounting Education and Research</u>, 11 (Fall 1975), 57-65.
The author examines some aspects of the accounting and control problems challenging the multinational firm.

Flint, David. "The Audit of Local Authority in Scotland." <u>The Accountant's Magazine</u>, 85 (August 1981), 257-258.
The author poses some pertinent questions raised by the House of Commons Public Accounts Committee on audits of local authority in Scotland.

Grollman, William K. "Independence of Auditors and Applicability to International Engagement." <u>The CPA Journal</u>, 43 (April 1973), 286-291.
This paper presents a brief description of the various re-

visions related to independence coupled with an analysis
relating the situation to international audit engagements.

Harding, Michael. "Problems of Obtaining Bank Confirmation
in Germany." Accountancy, 88 (August 1977), 88-89.
Auditors not resident in West Germany meet some resistance
from BDR banks to their confirmation requests. The author
examines the situation and offers some suggestions on how
to overcome the problems.

Hill, D.J. "Amendments to the Commonwealth Audit Act."
The Australian Accountant, 46 (July 1976), 355-356.
The author outlines the Audit Amendment Bill 1976, and notes
changes to the Audit Act 1901-1975.

Johnston, Donald J., W. Morley Lemon, and Frederick L. Neumann. "The Canadian Study of the Role of the Auditor."
Journal of Accounting, Auditing and Finance, 3 (Spring
1980), 251-263.
The purpose of this article is to outline some of the significant recommendations of the Canadian report and to point
out some of those similarities to, as well as some differences from, its American counterpart.

Keyserlingk, Alexander N. "International Public Accounting:
An Underdeveloped Profession." The International Journal
of Accounting Education and Research, 11 (Fall 1975), 15-22.
The author feels that if the long-range view is not taken,
there will continue to be an underdeveloped accounting profession in many countries.

Kullberg, Duane R. "Management of a Multinational Public
Accounting Firm." The International Journal of Accounting
Education and Research, 17 (Fall 1981), 1-6.
This article outlines the management of a multinational ac-
counting firm--Arthur Andersen--by its managing partner.

Lee, Marikay. "The International Auditor." The Internal
Auditor, 35 (December 1978), 43-47.
This article is concerned with how to perform audits on the
international scene. The author has performed audits in
Canada, Mexico, Brazil, Panama, Jamaica, Trinidad, Bel-
gium, Holland, and Germany.

Louwers, Pieter C. "The European Public Accountant: A
Different View." Management Accounting, 57 (September
1975), 43-46.
This is a critique of Professor Crum's article which appeared in the March 1975 issue of Management Accounting.

Mann, Richard W., and Derek H. Redmayne. "Internal Auditing in an International Environment." The Internal Auditor, 36 (October 1979), 49-54.
Performing international audits presents unique problems, and the authors explain them and related opportunities.

Markell, William. "A Comparison of Preparation for the Accounting Profession Among New Zealand, the United Kingdom, and the United States." The International Journal of Accounting Education and Research, 15 (Spring 1980), 101-114.
This paper deals with the many differences that exist between New Zealand, the UK and the US related to admission to the profession, and the education system.

Marshall, A. John. "Public Accounting & Multinationalism." CA Magazine, 105 (December 1974), 35-40.
The author feels that firms would benefit greatly if the accounting profession could develop some cooperation between professional bodies in both developed and developing nations.

Moonitz, Maurice. "International Auditing Standards: A Reply." The Accountant's Magazine, 83 (April 1979), 156.
In an article in the February 1979 issue of The Accountant's Magazine Jack Shaw reviewed International Auditing Standards, the recently published book by Edward Stamp and Maurice Moonitz. In this article Professor Moonitz replies to some of the issues raised in the February article.

Moore, David. "Auditing the EEC." Accountancy, 90 (September 1979), 59-62.
This article rectifies the first annual report of the European Court of Auditors published by the EEC and explains what the Court does and why it is needed.

Parker, John W. "International Auditing: A Case History." The Internal Auditor, 32 (November/December 1975), 63-66.
This article tells how one corporation met the challenges of organizing and conducting international audits.

Pomeranz, Felix. "International Auditing Standards." The International Journal of Accounting Education and Research, 11 (Fall 1975), 1-13.
The author examines the history of auditing, and gives consideration to the standards that exist in various countries in the areas of independence and audit procedures. Then a case study is discussed.

Richards, William R. "Auditing U.S. Companies With Operations Abroad." The International Journal of Accounting Education and Research, 12 (Fall 1976), 1-12.
This article deals with the problems encountered in auditing U.S. companies with operations abroad. It includes also a discussion of the differences between auditing standards in the U.S. and those of other countries.

Robertson, Ian C.M. "Audit Committees in the United Kingdom." The Accountant's Magazine, 80 (August 1976), 287-289.
This article discusses the establishment of audit committees as a normal part of United Kingdom business practice, and examines some of the benefits which can flow from a well run audit committee.

Schwartz, Ivo. "The Harmonisation of Accounting and Auditing in the European Community." The Accountant's Magazine, 81 (December 1977), 508-510.
This article is concerned with the subject of harmonisation of auditing and accounting standards from the point of view of the European Community.

Shaw, J.C. "International Auditing Standards." The Accountant's Magazine, 83 (February 1979), 55-57.
This article is a preliminary review of a book by Edward Stamp and Maurice Moonitz entitled, International Auditing Standards. In this review, a number of the important and interesting issues raised by the authors are considered.

Tipgos, Manuel A. "Potential Liabilities in International Accounting Practice." The Journal of Accountancy, 151 (April 1981), 24-30.
The author explores ways the U.S. accounting profession can counteract the threat of legal liabilities associated with international practice, and the extent to which principal auditors are liable is substandard work is performed by a foreign correspondent auditor.

Tooman, Lee D. "Starting the Internal Audit of Foreign Operations." The Internal Auditor, 32 (November/December 1975), 56-62.
The purpose of this article is to provide some general information that may be helpful in answering some of the more basic questions involved in starting international audits.

Weinstein, Arnold K., Louis Corsini, and Ronald Pawliczek. "The Big Eight in Europe." The International Journal of Accounting Education and Research, 13 (Spring 1978), 57-72.
This paper analyzes the organizational structures utilized

by the Big Eight in Europe and seeks to identify the operational impact of these structures.

Wesberry, James P., Jr. "Are International Standards Possible?" The Internal Auditor, 35 (December 1978), 36–42. The latest step in the growth of the internal audit profession is formal approval of the final draft of the Standards for the Professional Practice of Internal Auditing. The author discusses whether these standards are applicable on a worldwide basis.

Wu, Frederick H., and Donald W. Hackett. "The Internationalization of U.S. Public Accounting Firms: An Empirical Study." The International Journal of Accounting Education and Research, 12 (Spring 1977), 81–92. The objective of this research is to determine the progress of U.S. public accounting firms' foreign expansion, the procedures used in establishing these operations, and the problems encountered in the process of internationalization.

The Foreign Corrupt Practices Act

Ballinger, Edward, and Jesse F. Dillard. "The Foreign Corrupt Practices Act." The CPA Journal, 50 (February 1980), 37–46. The authors present a thorough analysis of the Foreign Corrupt Practices Act of 1977, and the associated regulations proposed and promulgated by the SEC.

Baruch, Hurd. "The Foreign Corrupt Practices Act." Harvard Business Review, 57 (January-February 1979), 32–51. The author explains the Foreign Corrupt Practices Act and how the SEC is likely to interpret its meaning.

Basche, James. "Questionable Payments and Regulation of Multinational Corporations." Journal of Contemporary Business, 6 (Autumn 1977), 165–177. The author discusses several types of questionable payments, and some ways of regulating the practice.

Benjamin, James J., Paul E. Dascher, and Robert G. Morgan. "How Corporate Controllers View the Foreign Corrupt Practices Act." Management Accounting, 60 (June 1979), 43–45, 49. This article describes the provisions of the Foreign Corrupt Practices Act and the role that the controller has to play to prevent the severe penalties of this Act.

61

Beresford, Dennis R., and James D. Bond. "The Foreign Corrupt Practices Act--Its Implication to Financial Management." Financial Executive, 46 (August 1978), 26-33.
This article summarizes the main provisions of the Foreign
Corrupt Practices Act, specially the provision related to
the corporate code of conduct developed to prevent bribes
as well as the auditor's responsibility.

Block, Dennis J., and Ellen J. O'Doner. "Enforcing The
Accounting Standards Provisions of the Foreign Corrupt
Practices Act." Financial Executive, 47 (July 1979), 19-26.
This article discusses the SEC's present enforcement posture with respect to the accounting standards provisions of
the Act, how the new rules may affect that posture, and how
management should respond when it becomes aware of conduct
that may violate the Act and these rules.

Bradt, John D. "The Foreign Corrupt Practices Act and the
Internal Auditor." The Internal Auditor, 36 (August 1979),
15-20.
The author explains the internal auditor's role in relation
to the Foreign Corrupt Practices Act.

Carmichael, D.R. "Internal Accounting Control--It's The
Law." The Journal of Accountancy, 149 (May 1980), 70-76.
The author discusses the FCPA and its so-called standards
which establish requirements for accurate accounting records
and sound internal accounting control.

Chazen, Charles. "An Accountant Looks at the FCPA." The
CPA Journal, 50 (May 1980), 38-45.
The author explores and comments on the problems of the CPA
in reporting under the Foreign Corrupt Practices Act. Emphasis is placed on the effects of related SEC rules and
proposed rules on the auditor.

Hinsey, Joseph. "The Foreign Corrupt Practices Act--The
Legislation As Enacted." Financial Executive, 47 (July
1979), 12-18.
This article briefly summarizes the foreign bribery provisions of the Act.

Holt, Robert N., and Rebecca E. Fincher. "The Foreign Corrupt Practices Act." Financial Analysts Journal, 37 (March/
April 1981), 73-76.
This article outlines the main provisions of the FCPA and
its effect on business, accountants and auditors.

Kaikati, Jack, and Wayne A. Label. "The Foreign Antibri-

bery Law: Friend or Foe?" <u>Columbia Journal of World Business</u>, 15 (Spring 1980), 46-51.
This article presents some key aspects of the Foreign Corrupt Practices Act and their implications for the accounting profession and multinational executives.

Kim, Suk H. "On Repealing the Foreign Corrupt Practices Act: Survey and Assessment." <u>Columbia Journal of World Business</u>, 16 (Fall 1981), 16-21.
The author recently surveyed members of <u>Fortune</u> 500 firms to answer one question: Should the Act be repealed?

Kline, John. "Entrapment or Opportunity: Structuring A Corporate Response to International Codes of Conduct." <u>Columbia Journal of World Business</u>, 15 (Summer 1980), 6-13.
The author points out that MNCs can expect a proliferation of "voluntary" international codes of conduct as governments seek diplomatic harmony without incurring real policy harmonization costs.

Maher, Michael W. "The Impact of Regulation on Controls: Firms' Response to the Foreign Corrupt Practices Act." <u>The Accounting Review</u>, 56 (October 1981), 751-770.
This paper presents a conceptual and empirical analysis of how coalitions of managers respond to regulation.

Marsh, Hugh L. "The Foreign Corrupt Practices Act: A Corporate Plan for Compliance." <u>The Internal Auditor</u>, 36 (April 1979), 72-76.
The author outlines the action-oriented approach a major US based MNC has taken to ensure compliance with the FCPA.

McKee, Thomas E. "Auditing Under the Foreign Corrupt Practices Act." <u>The CPA Journal</u>, 49 (August 1979), 31-36.
The Foreign Corrupt Practices Act of 1977 and its impact on internal and external auditors are reviewed.

McQueary, Glen M. II, and Michael P. Risdon. "How We Comply With the Foreign Corrupt Practices Act." <u>Management Accounting</u>, 61 (November 1979), 39-43.
Two corporate auditors tell how their company devised a complete internal control system to comply with the provisions of the Foreign Corrupt Practices Act.

Merten, Alan G., Dennis G. Severance, and Bernard J. White. "Internal Control and the Foreign Corrupt Practices Act." <u>Sloan Management Review</u>, 22 (Spring 1981), 47-54.
The authors report the results of a survey of top corporate officers from nearly 700 firms representing a broad cross-

section of industry types and company sizes.

Neumann, Frederick L. "Corporate Audit Committees and the Foreign Corrupt Practices Act." The Journal of Accountancy, 151 (March 1981), 78-80.
The author discusses the role of the corporate audit committee in overseeing management's compliance with the Foreign Corrupt Practices Act.

Norgaard, Corine T., and William W. Granow. "Internal Auditing's Response to the Foreign Corrupt Practices Act." The Internal Auditor, 36 (December 1979), 54-64.
This article describes the impact of the FCPA on the internal audit staffs of large industrial corporations.

Reavell, Fraser M. "The US 'Foreign Bribery' Act Gives Headaches to Accountants." Accountancy, 91 (September 1980), 58-60.
The author explains that the US Foreign Corrupt Practices Act has significant implications for auditors and accountants in the UK as well as the US.

Ricchiute, David N. "Foreign Corrupt Practices: A New Responsibility for Internal Auditors." The Internal Auditor, 35 (December 1978), 58-64.
The author explains the internal auditor's role concerning foreign corrupt practices.

Sumutka, Alan R. "Questionable Payment and Practices: Why? How? Detection? Prevention." The Journal of Accountancy, 149 (March 1980), 50-64.
The author concludes that outright detection and prevention of illegal activities appear unlikely unless corporations comply with the accurate recordkeeping provision of the Foreign Corrupt Practices Act of 1977.

MANAGEMENT ACCOUNTING ISSUES

Challenges for Managerial Accountants

Berry, Maureen H. "Why International Cost Accounting Practices Should Be Harmonized." Management Accounting, 63 (August 1981), 36-42.
The author points out that countries involved in coproduction ventures need a mutually agreeable method of resolving their cost-sharing problems.

Choi, Frederick D.S. "Multinational Challenges for Managerial Accountants." Journal of Contemporary Business, 4 (Autumn 1975), 51-67.
This paper identifies some of the problem areas and issues which the MNC is posing for managerial accountants.

Enthoven, Adolf J.H. "International Management Accounting--A Challenge for Accountants." Management Accounting, 62 (September 1980), 25-32.
The rise of the MNC has forced changes in the nature and techniques of international management accounting. This article describes some of these changes.

Multinational Corporate Pricing

Arpan, Jeffrey S. "Multinational Firm Pricing in International Markets." Sloan Management Review, 14 (Winter 1972/73), 1-11.
This paper contains a summary of research performed on certain elements of the pricing practices of MNCs.

Belli, Pedro. "Comments on 'Multinational corporate Pricing Policy in the Developing Countries.'" Journal of International Business Studies, 8 (Spring/Summer 1977), 99-102.
This comment is in reference to Nathaniel Leff's article entitled "Multinational Corporate Pricing Strategy in Developing Countries," that appeared in the Fall 1975 issue of this journal.

Jagpal, Harsharanjeet Singh. "A Note on 'Multinational Corporate Pricing Policy in the Developing Countries.'" Journal of International Business Studies, 8 (Spring/Summer 1977), 103-104.
This comment is in reference to Nathaniel Leff's article that appeared in the Fall 1975 issue of this journal.

Leff, Nathaniel H. "Multinational Corporate Pricing Policy

in the Developing Countries." <u>Journal of International Business Studies</u>, 6 (Fall 1975), 55–64.
This paper suggests a new look at corporate pricing in developing countries. Because of conditions discussed in the paper, the price elasticity of demand curves in individual markets may be much greater than companies assume. A shift to a low price/high volume may both increase profits and satisfy social needs to which host country governments are sensitive.

Leff, Nathaniel H. "Multinational Corporate Pricing Policy in the Developing Countries: A Reply." <u>Journal of International Business Studies</u>, 8 (Spring/Summer 1977), 105–106.
This is Nathaniel Leff's reply to the comments made in the same issue of this journal by Pedro Belli and Harsharanjeet Singh Jagpal on this article which appeared in the Fall 1975 issue of this journal.

Investing and Financing Decisions

Adler, Michael, and Bernard Dumas. "Optimal International Acquisitions." <u>The Journal of Finance</u>, 30 (March 1975), 1–19.
This paper aims to innovate by using the theory of capital asset pricing to extend the theory of conglomerate acquisitions to the international setting.

Adler, Michael. "Investor Recognition of Corporation International Diversification: Comment." <u>The Journal of Finance</u>, 36 (March 1981), 187–190.
The purpose of this article is to comment on a paper by T. Agmon and D. Lessard entitled, "Investor Recognition of Corporate International Diversification," published in <u>The Journal of Finance</u> (September 1977),

Aggarwal, Raj. "Multinationality and Stock Market Valuation: An Empirical Study of U.S. Markets and Companies." <u>Management International Review</u>, 19 (1979/2), 5–22.
This paper provides empirical evidence regarding the stock market valuation of multinationality. The results of this study indicate that in the U.S. increasing multinationality is correlated with decreasing systematic risk and an increasing price-to-earning ratio.

Agmon, Tamir, and Donald R. Lessard. "Investor Recognition of Corporate International Diversification." <u>The Journal of Finance</u>, 32 (September 1977), 1049–1055.
This paper argues that barriers to portfolio capital flows

do exist, and provides empirical support for the diversification motive by showing that investors appear to recognize the extent of multinational diversification of a sample of U.S. firms listed on the New York Stock Exchange.

Agmon, Tamir, and Donald Lessard. "Investor Recognition of Corporation International Diversification: Comment." The Journal of Finance, 36 (March 1981), 191-192.
This is Professors Agmon and Lessard's reply to the comments made by Professor Michael Adler in this same issue.

Anderson, A.G. "Development Finance: A Personal View." The Accountant's Magazine, 81 (October 1977), 428-429.
The author gives his views on what development finance is, and describes how it works in the context of a "devco" (development finance corporation) in a less developed country.

Baker, James C., and L.J. Beardsley. "Capital Budgeting by U.S. Multinational Companies." The Financial Review, 2 (1972), 115-121.
This paper is concerned primarily with which of several capital budgeting techniques is the most practical for evaluating competing capital projects both for initial investments and for expansion or modernization by a MNC.

Bardsley, R. Geoffrey. "Managing International Financial Transactions." The International Journal of Accounting Education and Research, 8 (Fall 1972), 67-76.
The author presents an outline of international financial management from the treasurer's office point of view by looking at the problems, objectives, policies and practices.

Bavishi, Vinod B. "Capital Budgeting Practices at Multinationals." Management Accounting, 63 (August 1981), 32-35.
This article reports the results of a survey to the top financial executives of the 306 largest U.S. based MNCs as to their capital budgeting practices.

Bennett, J.W. "Capital Expenditure Evaluation in a Multinational Business." The Australian Accountant, 51 (November 1981), 673-675.
The author describes a capital expenditure plan for a multinational business.

Black, Fischer. "The Ins and Outs of Foreign Investments." Financial Analysts Journal, 34 (May/June 1978), 25-32.
This article lays out the basic economic influences on investments across national boundaries.

Bloch, Henry Simon. "Export Financing Emerging As a Major Policy Problem." Columbia Journal of World Business, 11 (Fall 1976), 85-95.
The author takes a hard look at the politics and economics of export financing. In arguing for long-term export insurance for trade with LDCs, he reveals the counter-productive effects of export subsidies and import restriction, and suggests that the Export-Import Bank be reconstructed so as to better service long-term objectives.

Choi, Frederick D.S. "Multinational Financing and Accounting Harmony." Management Accounting, 55 (March 1974), 14-17.
The author indicates that international disclosure standards are indeed feasible. He also offers a technique by which a "disclosure score" may be derived from a company's annual report.

Choi, Frederick D.S. "Multinational Finance and Management Accounting." Management Accounting, 58 (October 1976), 45-48.
The author describes some of the issues facing international financial managers and the accounting implications of those issues such as the problem of avoiding foreign exchange risks, consolidation, taxation, capital budgeting, financial control systems, and external financing.

Cinnamon, Allan. "Why Foreign Investment in the UK Can Be Worthwhile." Accountancy, 89 (January 1978), 82-85.
The overseas businessman too often has the impression that in setting up a UK enterprise he will lock himself into a highly-taxed territory, frozen in by exchange controls. The author argues that effective rates of UK tax can be minimal, and tax profits may be freely repatriated with little exchange control formality.

Cohn, Richard A., and John J. Pringle. "Imperfections in International Financial Markets: Implications for Risk Premia and the Cost of Capital to Firms." The Journal of Finance, 28 (March 1973), 59-66.
The purpose of this paper is to examine several theoretical implications of international diversification, with particular attention to the effects of imperfections in international financial markets on risk premia for capital assets, the cost of capital to firms, and the efficiency with which capital is allocated.

DaCosta, Richard C., James Fisher, and William M. Lawson. "Linkages in the International Business Community: Accoun-

ting Evidence." <u>Journal of International Business Studies</u>, 11 (Fall 1980), 92-102.
This article investigates the existence of international linkages in the business community through reference to accounting practices by testing two hypotheses which focus on linkages between accounting practices and the information needs of the financial community in different countries.

Davis, Steven I. "How Risky is International Lending?" <u>Harvard Business Review</u>, 55 (January-February 1977), 135-143.
The author suggests that the risks in the field of international lending are not really any greater than in domestic lending.

Dawson, Steven M. "Eurobond Currency Selection: Hindsight." <u>Financial Executive</u>, 41 (November 1973), 72-73.
The author points out that the environment of domestic markets is radically altered in the Eurobond market, where exchange rate adjustments can produce large increases in expected costs.

Drury, D.H. "Accounting Risk Associations of Internationally Interlisted Firms." <u>Management International Review</u>, 17 (1977/3), 53-64.
The reaction by international and national investors to publicly reported corporate reporting are examined. The study shows that international investors prefer detailed financial information and domestic investors desire summary figures.

Dyment, John J. "International Cash Management." <u>Harvard Business Review</u>, 56 (May-June 1978), 143-150.
The author draws on the experiences of some companies that he is aware of to aid other managements in analyzing their cash receipts and disbursement systems, and their relationship with banks.

Errunza, Vihang R., and Lemma W. Senbet. "The Effects of International Operations On The Market Value of the Firm: Theory and Evidence." <u>The Journal of Finance</u>, 36 (May 1981), 401-418, 439-440.
This paper investigates the existence of monopoly rents associated with international operations in a market-value theoretical framework.

Findlay, M. Chapman III, and Elko J. Kleinschmidt. "Error-Learning in the Eurodollar Market." <u>Journal of Financial and Quantitative Analysis</u>, 10 (September 1975), 429-446.

This paper begins the task of filling the empirical gap of knowledge about the term structure of Eurodollar deposit rates. Specifically, the authors test the hypothesis that the market does behave as though it predicts future interest rates, such that the forward rates impounded in the term structure are a function of expected future rates.

Finney, M.J. "Euro-Sterling Issues." The Accountant, 178 (1 June 1978), 732-734.
This article is concerned with financing of international activities of multinationals. The author discusses tax and exchange control factors of Euro-sterling bond issues.

Fisk, Charles, and Frank Rimlinger. "Nonparametric Estimates of LDC Repayment Prospects." The Journal of Finance, 34 (May 1979), 429-436.
This paper presents a procedure for estimating which countries will reschedule their debts. Details of the procedure are presented, historical tests of the procedure are shown, then results of the tests are summarized.

Folks, William R., Jr. "Optimal Foreign Borrowing Strategies with Operations in Forward Exchange Markets." Journal of Financial and Quantitative Analysis, 13 (June 1978), 245-254.
The purpose of this paper is to find the optimal currency source or sources for a loan to a unit of a MNC when the borrowing unit can enter the forward exchange market for a term equivalent to the time to maturity of the loan.

Folks, William R., Jr., and Ramesh Advani. "Raising Funds With Foreign Currency." Financial Executive, 48 (February 1980), 44-49.
The authors have developed an evaluation technique for determining the best currency of denomination for issuance of fixed interest rate securities from the issuer's standpoint. This method, the Interest Cost Technique, develops a cost measure for each financing alternative, and compares these costs to determine the desired currency of denomination.

Fung, W.K.H. "Gains from International Portfolio Diversification: A Comment." Journal of Business Finance & Accounting, 6 (Spring 1979), 45-49.
The author comments on an article by A. Saunders and R. Woodward which appeared in the Autumn 1977 issue of this journal. An alternative approach for demonstrating the gains from international portfolio diversification is tested on the data presented in SW.

Goeltz, Richard K. "Managing Liquid Funds Internationally." Columbia Journal of World Business, 7 (July-August
1972), 59-65.
The author discusses ways in which the financial managers
of MNCs are utilizing non-traditional techniques in their
international cash management systems.

Gregor, William T., J.C. Kirby, S.M. Robbins, and R.B. Stobaugh. "Changes in International Capital Market." Financial Executive, 42 (November 1974), 50-62.
This article describes changes in the international capital market which the authors say have created a spectre of
uncertainty, causing a reluctance of lenders to accept risk.

Guy, James R.F. "An Examination of the Effects of International Diversification From the British Viewpoint on Both
Hypothetical and Real Portfolios." The Journal of Finance,
33 (December 1978), 1425-1438.
This study examines the cost of exchange controls and their
effect on the potential benefits of international diversification, examines how a sample of internationally diversified British closed-end investment trusts performed within
the institutional environment of the sixties.

Hallett, David. "Investment by Institutions in the United
States." The Accountant, 182 (3/10 January 1980), 16-19.
This article deals with investment in the US by UK insti-
tutions, rather than individuals.

Hockey, Paul. "Use of Link Companies for UK/US Investment." The Accountant, 182 (17 January 1980), 57-59.
This article examines the use of link companies for US corporations to invest in the UK and for UK companies to invest
in the US.

Hunter, Robert L., Gary M. Cunningham, and Thomas G. Evans.
"Are Multinational Liquidity Models Worth Their Cost?"
Management Accounting, 61 (December 1979), 51-56.
The authors examine liquidity allocation devices and other
factors related to the models developed for that purpose.
Based on that examination, they question whether mathema-
tical optimization models can ever achieve the returns ex-
pected.

Jucker, James V., and Clovis de Faro. "The Selection of
International Borrowing Sources." Journal of Financial and
Quantitative Analysis, 10 (September 1975), 381-407.
The purpose of this article is to develop a method for
evaluating and selecting international borrowing sources

in the face of exchange rate uncertainties.

Kitching, John. "Winning and Losing With European Acquisitions." Harvard Business Review, 52 (March-April 1974), 124-136.
This article, based on extensive personal experience and on a survey, plots the course for a successful acquisition program.

Kramer, Gerald. "Borrowing on the International Capital Markets." Columbia Journal of World Business, 9 (Spring 1974), 73-77.
In analyzing the choice of what is least expensive ultimately, one should be wary of low interest rates and try to borrow in weak currencies. This general rule can be ignored, however, depending on the purpose for which the borrowing will be made and the different currencies generated throughout the income stream of the MNC.

Lee, Boyden E. "The Euro-Dollar Multiplier." The Journal of Finance, 28 (September 1973), 867-874.
This paper contends that the stock of net Euro-dollar deposits can be expressed as the product of a Euro-dollar base and a Euro-dollar multiplier. As in domestic models, the terms of the multiplier reflect asset choices of the sectors reflected by them.

Lessard, Donald R. "International Portfolio Diversification: A Multivariate Analysis for a Group of Latin American Countries." The Journal of Finance, 28 (June 1973), 619-633.
This article examines international diversification potential among a set of developing countries and determines the feasibility of creating investment unions which provide diversification benefits while meeting the political requirements of participants.

Lessard, Donald R. "International Diversification." Financial Analysts Journal, 32 (January/February 1976), 32-38.
The author points out that because a few large countries represent the bulk of the market value in the world portfolio, they contribute importantly to its overall risk.
In an integrated world capital market, any portfolio that ducks its full share of the risk specific to these countries will suffer a disproportionate sacrifice in expected return.

Levin, Jay H. "A Financial Sector Analysis of the Eurodollar Market." The Journal of Finance, 29 (March 1974), 103-117.

The Gramley-Chase-Smith financial sector model is reviewed and modified, then extended to include Eurodollar transactions. An alternative model of the Eurodollar market is presented in which Regulation Q ceilings are imposed on U.S. time deposit rates, and results are summarized.

Lloyd, William P., Steven J. Goldstein, and Robert B. Rogow. "International Portfolio Diversification of Real Assets: An Update." Journal of Business Finance & Accounting, 8 (Spring 1981), 45-50.
The purpose of this study is to update with more recent data previous investigations that note the potential for gains from international diversification.

Malkoff, Alan R. "Foreign Acquisition Analysis: A Suggested Approach." Management Accounting, 60 (June 1979), 32-36, 41.
The author suggests an approach for reviewing and analyzing foreign acquisition candidates and currency exposure in a systematic manner. The overall process has been separated into investment and financing decisions.

Mazzolini, Renato. "Creating Europe's Multinationals: The International Merger Route." The Journal of Business, 48 (January 1975), 39-51.
Due to a host of obstacles, international mergers have been quite rare. This paper examines these obstacles and points to possible solutions.

Mehra, Rajnish. "On the Financing and Investment Decisions of Multinational Firms in the Presence of Exchange Risk." Journal of Financial and Quantitative Analysis, 13 (June 1978), 227-244.
This paper, with the aid of a two-country model, attempts to investigate the effects of exchange risk on the investment and financing decisions of multinational firms.

Naumann-Etienne, Ruediger. "A Framework for Financial Decisions in Multinational Corporations--Summary of Recent Research." Journal of Financial and Quantitative Analysis, 9 (November 1974), 859-874.
This paper, which restricts its analysis to U.S. MNCs, reviews the major aspects of an appropriate normative framework for financial decisions in the MNC.

Ness, Walter L. "A Linear Programming Approach To Financing the Multinational Corporation." Financial Management, 1 (Winter 1972), 88-100.
This article develops a linear programming model for finan-

cing MNCs. The model used in this article assumes that the transfer of funds from one subsidiary to another will be done by the transfer method which implies the lowest cost for each alternative source of finance and that all available funds can be transferred by that method.

Obersteiner, Erich. "Should the Foreign Affiliate Remit Dividends or Reinvest?" Financial Management, 2 (Spring 1973), 88-93.
The author develops a general decision model for the optimal allocation of foreign generated funds to the alternatives of foreign dividend remittances and foreign investment.

Obersteiner, Erich. "The Management of Liquid Fund Flows Across National Boundaries." The International Journal of Accounting Education and Research, 11 (Spring 1976), 91-101.
The decision problems of international fund flows within the constraints of a MNC are examined and a rational approach to the solution of such problems is suggested.

Oblak, David J., and Roy J. Helm, Jr. "Survey and Analysis of Capital Budgeting Methods Used by Multinationals." Financial Management, 9 (Winter 1980), 37-41.
This paper reports the results of a 1979 survey of capital budgeting procedures used by 58 U.S.-based MNCs.

Phillips, J.D.W. "Exchange Control Hazards." Accountancy, 85 (August 1974), 68-70.
The author examines the problems of exchange control and the dollar premium brought about by regulations governing foreign investment.

Prindl, Andreas. "Multinational Finance." Accountancy, 85 (December 1974), 82-85.
The principal difficulties of financial controls in MNCs are discussed.

Prindl, Andreas R. "Guidelines for MNC Money Managers." Harvard Business Review, 54 (January-February 1976), 73-80.
The author discusses how MNCs should respond to unpredictable exchange markets and growing credit restrictions and describes how MNCs can strengthen their control system and techniques, augment their internal information systems, and lessen the impact of their fragmentation.

Remmers, H. Lee. "A Note On Foreign Borrowing Costs." Journal of International Business Studies, 11 (Fall 1980), 123-134.

This paper describes an alogorithm to estimate the effective after-tax cost of different short term debt or time deposit options available to foreign affiliates of MNCs.

Richards, Ferry E. "The Multinational Corporation's Borrowing Decision." Management Accounting, 57 (February 1976), 51-52.
Most foreign subsidiaries of American corporations are more highly levered than their parents. In this article, the American affiliate's criteria for borrowing and some of the limiting considerations are reviewed.

Robbins, Sidney M., and Robert B. Stobaugh, "Financing Foreign Affiliates." Financial Management, 1 (Winter 1972), 56-65.
The authors report the result of an empirical study of the financial practices of MNCs. They emphasize the misleading character of oft-quoted aggregated statistics, and report the results of a simulation demonstrating the tumultous character of fund flows within the frame of the multinational corporate network.

Robbins, Sidney M., and Robert B. Stobaugh. "Multinational Companies--Growth of the Financial Function." Financial Executive, 41 (July 1973), 24-31.
The authors describe three stages for the growth of the financial function of MNCs.

Robichek, Alexandre A., and Mark R. Eaker. "Debt Denomination and Exchange Risk in International Capital Market." Financial Management, 5 (Autumn 1976), 11-18.
The purpose of this article is to examine the wide range of international financial alternatives and to suggest ways of analyzing their potential value and/or risk to the firm.

Ryder, Frank R. "Challenges to the Use of the Documentary Credit in International Trade Transactions." Columbia Journal of World Business, 16 (Winter 1981), 36-41.
The documentary letter of credit has been useful in facilitating commercial transactions between buyers and sellers in different countries. However, these letters of credit are vulnerable to fraud and forgery. Another problem area is the exercise of local jurisdiction in settling disputes that arise under documentary credits.

Sangster, Bruce F. "International Funds Management." Financial Executive, 45 (December 1977), 46-52.
The author lays out an approach to international funds management that creates a set of objective decision aids

for the executive responsible for setting financial strategies.

Saunders, Anthony, and Richard S. Woodward. "Gains from International Portfolio Diversification: UK Evidence 1971-1975." Journal of Business Finance & Accounting, 4 (Autumn 1977), 299-309.
The history and operation of the UK investment premium is briefly described and a method of calculating premium adjusted returns presented. Then a comparison of the unadjusted and the adjusted returns on equity investment in seven major industrial countries is made, and some results are presented which test the optimality of "simple" investment decision rules for UK investors.

Saunders, Anthony, and Richard S. Woodward. "Gains from International Portfolio Diversification: A Reply." Journal of Business Finance & Accounting, 6 (Spring 1979), 51-2.
The authors defend their article published in the Autumn 1977 issue of this journal. This is in reply to a comment by W.K.H. Fung.

Scorey, Michael. "Eurobonds: Investments You're Not Supposed to Know About." Accountancy, 92 (January 1981), 48-50.
The author discusses the Eurobond market as a market for private investors.

Senbet, Lemma W. "International Capital Market Equilibrium and the Multinational Firm Financing and Investment Policies." Journal of Financial and Quantitative Analysis, 14 (September 1979), 455-480.
The purpose of this paper is to develop financing and investment policies for the MNC in the framework of international capital equilibrium. The analysis incorporates foreign exchange rate fluctuation, differential international interest rates, and differential international taxes.

Severn, Alan K., and David R. Meinster. "The Use of Multicurrency Financing by the Financial Manager." Financial Management, 7 (Winter 1978), 45-53.
This paper examines, from the financial manager's viewpoint, the risk and cost of bonds denominated in Special Drawing Right (SDR), which consists of specified amounts of 16 major currencies.

Shapiro, Alan C. "Evaluating Financing Costs For Multinational Subsidiaries." Journal of International Business Studies, 6 (Fall 1975), 25-32.

This paper presents a methodology for determining the true costs of alternative sources of financing for the MNC when the risk of exchange rate changes is present and different tax rates and regulations are in effect.

Shapiro, Alan C. "International Cash Management--The Determination of Multicurrency Cash Balances." Journal of Financial and Quantitative Analysis, 11 (December 1976), 893-900.
This paper extends the traditional single-currency deterministic cash balance model, developed by Baumol, to the multicurrency cash where payments and receipts are denominated in several currencies. The effect of foreign exchange risk on cash management policies is also analyzed.

Shapiro, Alan C. "Capital Budgeting for the Multinational Corporation." Financial Management, 7 (Spring 1978), 7-16.
The author states that capital budgeting for the MNC presents many problems that rarely if ever exist in domestic capital budgeting. This paper examines such problems and suggests ways to cope with them by adjusting cash flows instead of the cost of capital.

Shapiro, Alan C. "Financial Structure and Cost of Capital in the Multinational Corporation." Journal of Financial and Quantitative Analysis, 13 (June 1978), 211-226.
This paper seeks to provide a comprehensive approach to analyze the cost-of-capital question.

Shapiro, Alan C. "Payments Netting In International Cash Management." Journal of International Business Studies, 9 (Fall 1978), 51-58.
The purpose of this paper is to show how mathematical programming can be used to design a netting system capable of minimizing the total costs involved in settling interaffiliate accounts.

Shen, Paul. "Cash Flow Budgeting for the Importer." Management Accounting, 62 (September 1980), 33-35.
Importers encounter unusual cash flow problems. Even though sales for an importer may be up in any given period, accounts receivable may not be paid immediately. The importer's difficulties include the problem of foreign exchange rate fluctuation. The author outlines a strategy for solving these problems.

Solnik, B.H. "The International Pricing of Risk: An Empirical Investigation of the World Capital Market Structure." The Journal of Finance, 29 (May 1974), 365-378.

This paper attempts to determine the international market structure of asset prices, and an empirical examination of two market specifications of international price behavior is presented.

Solnik, Bruno H. "Why Not Diversify Internationally Rather Than Domestically?" Financial Analysts Journal, 30 (July-August 1974), 48-54.
The purpose of this article is to show that substantial advantages in risk reduction can be attained through portfolio diversification in foreign securities as well as in domestic common stocks.

Stockton, K.J. "Borrowing Foreign Currency." The Australian Accountant, 49 (December 1979), 769-773.
This article describes the factors that have to be taken into consideration in making decisions regarding borrowing from outside the country. It also points out the cost and risk involved in borrowing foreign currency and the role that foreign banks could play.

Stulz, René M. "On The Effects of Barriers To International Investment." The Journal of Finance, 36 (September 1981), 923-934.
This paper constructs a model of international asset pricing in which there is a cost associated with holding--either long or short--risky foreign securities.

Turner, J. Horsfall. "The Eurocurrency Loan." Accountancy, 85 (August 1974), 64-66.
The author considers the legal aspects that arise when a company turns to the Eurocurrency markets for financing.

Van Cise, Jerrold G. "Antitrust Guides to Foreign Acquisitions." Harvard Business Review, 50 (November-December 1972), 82-88.
An acquisition in the foreign sector poses legal problems that are not always present in domestic mergers. The author offers advice on horizontal, vertical, and other types of mergers, as well as joint ventures.

Watson, J. "A Study of Possible Gains from International Investment." Journal of Business Finance & Accounting, 5 (Summer 1978), 195-206.
The purpose of this study is to test the hypothesis that by international diversification, the investor can eliminate that part of the portfolio risk associated with the economics of a particular country.

Wooster, John T., and G. Richard Thoman. "New Financial
Priorities for MNCs." Harvard Business Review, 52 (May-
June 1974), 58-68.
This article describes new and sophisticated techniques
that MNCs can use to maintain their profit positions, and
also analyzes the forces that will shape the management of
international finance in the future.

Wundisch, Karl. "Centralized Cash Management Systems for
the Multinational Enterprise." Management International
Review, 13 (1973/6), 43-57.
After describing some of the techniques in use by MNEs which
are employed to minimize the opportunity cost of idle, mis-
located, and misdirected cash, and exploring the changing
attitude of the multinational banks, an attempt is made to
delineate an Optimum Decision Model for the assistance of
the cash management team of the MNE.

Financial Risk Management

Abdel-Malek, Talaat. "Managing Exchange Risks Under
Floating Rates: The Canadian Experience." Columbia Journal
of World Business, 11 (Fall 1976), 41-52.
In this article, the managerial implications of alternative
risk policies are examined. The author identifies and
evaluates critical factors affecting exchange risk management in a sample of Canadian firms under floating rates.

Adler, Michael, and Bernard Dumas. "The Exposure of Long-
Term Foreign Currency Bonds." Journal of Financial and
Quantitative Analysis, 15 (November 1980), 973-994.
This paper is concerned with the definition and determi-
nants of currency risk exposure.

Ankrom, Robert K. "Top-Level Approach to the Foreign Exchange Problem." Harvard Business Review, 52 (July-
August 1974), 79-90.
An experienced manager of international financing maintains
that, in the inevitable trade-offs between costs and risks,
only top management can decide on the best course for the
entire company.

Barnett, John S. "Corporate Foreign Exposure Strategy
Formulations." Columbia Journal of World Business, 11
(Winter 1976), 87-97.
The author investigates the increased awareness of the
fluctuations in foreign exposure by corporations and the
need to define a foreign exposure strategy to deal with

the problem, and develops a corporate strategy approach in a simplified and straightforward manner.

Batt, W.F.J. "Reducing Your Currency Risk." Accountancy, 85 (August 1974), 60–62.
The author discusses and evaluates the various methods of reducing currency risk.

Bhushan, Bhuwan. "Effects of Inflation and Currency Fluctuation." Management Accounting, 56 (July 1974), 17–19.
The author discusses various means of hedging, and illustrates the discussion with the case of an Argentine subsidiary.

Booth, G. Geoffrey, Fred R. Kaen, and Peter E. Koveos. "Currency Interdependence in Foreign Exchange Markets." The Financial Review, 15 (Fall 1980), 36–44.
The purpose of this paper is to investigate empirically the existence of long-term dependence in 91 exchange rate series. These series represent the rate of currency exchange between 14 pairs of countries.

Bowers, David A. "A Warning Note on Empirical Research Using Foreign Exchange Rates." Journal of Financial and Quantitative Analysis, 12 (June 1977), 315–319.
The author demonstrates that different points of view will give significantly different results from the same set of data. He shows that an analysis is sensitive to which currency of an exchange rate one chooses to make the numeraire.

Bradford, Samuel. "Managing Foreign Exchange." Accountancy, 86 (March 1975), 80–84.
This article explains how multinationals handle exchange risks. Several companies and the foreign currency translation methods they use are listed.

Bradford, Samuel R. "Foreign Exchange Exposure." Accountancy, 86 (September 1975), 74–78.
This article explains various methods of measuring foreign currency exchange exposure. The author concludes that there are limitations to the usefulness of each method.

Bradman, E.A. "Accounting for Foreign Exchange: Some Difficulties of Banks." The Accountant, 174 (1 January 1976), 6–8.
The author discusses problems arising in accounting for foreign exchange banks and in the determination of profits and losses from dealing in foreign currencies. He states

that some banks ignore results computed on outstanding forward contracts while others include them, and addresses the question of which treatment is more realistic.

Calderon-Rossell, Jorge R. "Covering Foreign Exchange Risks of Single Transactions: A Framework for Analysis." Financial Management, 8 (Autumn 1979), 78-85.
This article discusses some basic alternatives to protect the value of cash flows denominated in foreign currencies and introduces a general procedure to evaluate covering strategies for foreign exchange risk of single transactions.

Callier, Philippe. "Speculation and the Forward Foreign Exchange Rate: A Note." The Journal of Finance, 35 (March 1980), 173-176.
The author contends that, under the parity regime, speculation on the forward foreign exchange market is mainly the speculation on the future forward rate (for shorter contracts) expected to prevail before the maturity date of the speculative commitments of the speculators, who expect thus to be able to secure their speculative gains before the maturity date of the initial commitments.

Cornell, Bradford. "Inflation, Relative Price Changes, and Exchange Risk." Financial Management, 9 (Autumn 1980), 30-34.
This author claims that, once a firm takes account of inflation and relative price risk, no attention need be paid to exchange rates, and that the problems facing international firms are conceptually no different from those facing domestic firms.

Dufey, Gunter. "Corporate Finance and Exchange Rate Variations." Financial Management, 1 (Summer 1972), 51-58.
This article examines the current corporate policies to counter the effects of exchange rate changes. The author introduces a stage of analysis beyond immediate effect of balance sheet valuation changes.

Dufey, Gunter, and Rolf Mirus. "Forecasting Foreign Exchange Rates: A Pedagogical Note." Columbia Journal of World Business, 16 (Summer 1981), 53-61.
The authors analyze various methods used to forecast exchange rates and explain the reason why none of them can be expected to succeed in providing superior returns, appropriately measured.

Eaker, Mark R. "Covering Foreign Exchange Risks: Comment." Financial Management, 9 (Winter 1980), 64-65.

This comment identifies an error in a recent paper on alternative methods of hedging foreign exchange risk. Once the error is corrected, it is demonstrated that the choice of hedging technique depends on the validity of the interest rate parity theorem.

Eaker, Mark R. "Denomination Decisions for Multinational Transactions." Financial Management, 9 (Autumn 1980), 23-29.
This paper addresses the denomination decision for intra-company transactions. It demonstrates the impact of that decision on the firm and develops a decision rule for determining the preferred currency of denomination. A simulation is performed to provide some measure of the benefit to the firm of following that decision rule.

Eun, Choel S. "Global Purchasing Power View of Exchange Risk." Journal of Financial and Quantitative Analysis, 16 (December 1981), 639-650.
The main purpose of this paper is to investigate the nature of exchange risk based on a more general perception of international capital markets.

Evans, Thomas G. "Some Concerns About Exposure After the FASB's Statement No. 8." Financial Executive, 44 (November 1976), 28-31.
The purpose of this article is to point out the types of exposure risk that MNCs face and the different types of action they can consider for hedging this risk.

Everett, Robert M., Abraham M. George, and Aryeh Blumberg. "Appraising Currency Strengths and Weaknesses: An Operational Model for Calculating Parity Exchange Rates." Journal of International Business Studies, 11 (Fall 1980), 80-91.
This paper presents a model for appraising currencies that is based on an operational variant of purchasing power parity doctrine. The behavior of currencies under differing exchange regimes is analyzed in detail.

Ferchat, Robert. "Managing Foreign Exchange Risk." CA Magazine, 114 (January 1981), 26-28.
The author describes the effect of exchange rates on international pricing, and suggests a new approach to measuring foreign exchange exposure and developing a successful exposure draft including a sound financial communication scheme.

Feskoe, Gaffney. "Reducing Currency Risks in a Volatile

Foreign Exchange Market." Management Accounting, 62 (September 1980), 19-24.
This article outlines FAS No. 8 translation exposure, transaction or cash exposure, and consolidated earnings exposure. It also proposes a system of hedging these exposures.

Fletcher, John W. "Managing Foreign Exchange Risk." The Australian Accountant, 50 (August 1980), 450-455.
Changes in the international monetary system and options for reducing currency exposure are given by an expert of the Commonwealth Trading Bank of Australia.

Folks, William R., Jr. "Decision Analysis For Exchange Risk Management." Financial Management, 1 (Winter 1972), 101-112.
The purpose of this article is to develop relatively formal decision rules for managing the risk of exchange rate change. These rules are based on an analysis of a theoretical decision model of the exchange management process.

Folks, William R., Jr. "The Optimal Level of Forward Exchange Transactions." Journal of Financial and Quantitative Analysis, 8 (January 1973), 105-110.
This paper considers the problem of determining the optimal level of forward exchange purchases. The author shows that the decision maker's risk aversion characteristics determine the rate of change of the absolute level of speculation with respect to changes in wealth.

Folks, William R., Jr., and Stanley R. Stansell. "The Use of Discriminant Analysis in Forecasting." Journal of International Business Studies, 6 (Spring 1975), 33-50.
This paper presents the results of an exploratory survey of the applicability of discriminant analysis to the determination of medium-term exchange rate changes.

Fotheringham, K.B. "The Foreign Currency Hedge Market in Australia." The Australian Accountant, 49 (December 1979), 780-785.
This article describes developments that led to the need for hedging in the Australian economy, and the different methods available in the Australian economy for hedging.

Franck, Peter, and Allan Young. "Stock Price Reaction of Multinational Firms to Exchange Realignments." Financial Management, 1 (Winter 1972), 66-73.
The authors conclude that management firms with varying degrees of international activity should not expect the prices of their shares to reflect differences in the extent of

their international activity.

Frey, Karen M. "Management of Foreign Exchange Risk With Forward Contracts." Management Accounting, 58 (March 1977), 45-48.
The author contends that foreign exchange risk can be managed at modest cost using forward foreign contracts.

Friedman, Daniel. "Makin's MARP: A Comment." The Journal of Finance, 36 (June 1981), 739-742.
This is a comment on John Makin's article entitled, "Portfolio Theory and the Problem of Foreign Exchange Risk" in the May 1978 issue of this journal.

Giddy, Ian H. "Exchange Risk: Whose View?" Financial Management, 6 (Summer 1977), 23-33.
This paper contrasts the corporate treasurer's view of risk arising from currency fluctuations with the view of the manager of a foreign subsidiary and with that of the well-diversified shareholder.

Goodman, Stephen H. "Foreign Exchange-Rate Forecasting Techniques: Implications for Business and Policy." The Journal of Finance, 34 (May 1979), 415-427.
The purpose of this paper is to review and evaluate commercial services that provide foreign exchange rate forecasts and the techniques they use, and to consider the implications of the findings for business and policy.

Gull, Don S. "Composite Foreign Exchange Risk." Columbia Journal of World Business, 10 (Fall 1975), 51-69.
The author introduces the concept of Composite Foreign Exchange Risk, which deals with the statistical relationships among currencies and the risk associated with a portfolio of foreign exchange.

Gupta, Sanjeer. "A Note On the Efficiency of Black Markets In Foreign Currencies." The Journal of Finance, 36 (June 1981), 705-710.
The purpose of this article is to test the efficiency of the black market exchange rates in India, Taiwan, and South Korea.

Heckerman, Donald. "The Exchange Risks of Foreign Operations." The Journal of Business, 45 (January 1972), 42-48.
This article proposes a model based on present discounted value for measuring the exchange risk for firms that engage in foreign operations.

Hilley, John L., Carl R. Beidleman, and James A. Greenleaf. "Does Covered Interest Arbitrage Dominate in Foreign Exchange Markets?" Columbia Journal of World Business, 14 (Winter 1979), 99-107.
Using a direct measure of transaction costs involved in doing arbitrage in the foreign exchange market, the authors find little evidence of unexploited profit opportunities.

Hollis, Martha. "A Decentralized Foreign Exchange Risk Model." Management International Review, 20 (1980/3), 53-60.
This paper formulates the short-term money management problem with goals of matching maturing monetary assets and liabilities for each period in a multi-period horizon subject to policy and operating constraints. An illustration of the model is provided.

Hoyt, Newton H. "The Management of Currency Exchange Risk by the Singer Company." Financial Management, 1 (Spring 1972), 13-20.
This article outlines the problems related to exposure to foreign currency changes by multinationals. It also outlines some of the strategies that the Singer Company has adopted for hedging these risks.

Imai, Yutaka. "Exchange Rate Risk Protection in International Business." Journal of Financial and Quantitative Analysis, 10 (September 1975), 447-456.
This paper presents a way to incorporate the risk factor explicitly into the management of the exchange rate risk by applying portfolio theory.

Jacque, Laurent L. "Why Hedgers Are Not Speculators." Columbia Journal of World Business, 14 (Winter 1979), 108-116.
The author shows how firms can use their own risk-return tradeoffs in conjunction with known interdependencies among currencies to select the most appropriate hedging strategy.

Kahnamouyipour, Heydar. "Foreign Exchange Exposure Analysis." Accountancy, 90 (January 1979), 81-84.
The author proposes an analysis that avoids the need for some of the costly hedging.

Kahnamouyipour, Heydar. "Foreign Exchange: Hedge, Speculation, or Swap?" Accountancy, 91 (October 1980), 52-55.
This article discusses the accounting aspects of forward exchange deals.

Kettell, Brian. "Foreign Exchange Exposure." Accountancy, 89 (March 1978), 83-89.
The author explores some of the major issues in the debate about the relative merits of different accounting systems for translating financial statements, as seen from the different viewpoints of accountants and economists.

Kim, Seung H., and Paul J. Kuzdrall. "The Simulation of Financing Strategy Under Fluctuating Exchange Rate Conditions." The International Journal of Accounting Education and Research, 12 (Spring 1977), 93-108.
The authors present a simulation model to analyze instantaneously and accurately the effects of exchange rate changes experienced by a particular currency of a subsidiary company on the parent company's equity position.

Kohlhagen, Steven W. "Reducing Foreign Exchange Risks." Columbia Journal of World Business, 13 (Spring 1978), 33-38.
The author proposes a technique for dealing with exchange rate uncertainty that requires corporate officers to project a reasonable range over which rates might fluctuate.

Kohlhagen, Steven W. "A Model of Optimal Foreign Exchange Hedging Without Exchange Rate Projections." Journal of International Business Studies, 9 (Fall 1978), 9-19.
This article presents a technique for optimal hedging decisions for a general set of international financial problems, specifically within the context of a floating exchange rate regime.

Lasusa, Peter R. "Accounting for Hedged Transactions." The CPA Journal, 48 (June 1978), 17-24.
The purpose of this article is to describe the process of buying and selling hedges and to identify the relevant accounting pronouncements that should be considered in accounting for inventory where hedges are used.

Lieberman, Gail. "A Systems Approach to Foreign Exchange Risk Management." Financial Executive, 46 (December 1978), 14-19.
This article describes a systems approach to Foreign Exchange Risk Management which determines a company's actual foreign exchange risk position derived from an accounting treatment of foreign exchange gains and losses, and provides a structure to change actual data to evaluate alternative strategies.

Logue, Dennis E., and George S. Oldfield. "Managing Foreign Assets When Foreign Exchange Markets Are Efficient."

Financial Management, 6 (Summer 1977), 16-22.
This paper explores the influence of a firm hedging in an efficient foreign exchange market. The conclusion drawn is that hedging is irrelevant because the true value of currency fluctuations is reflected in security prices.

Makin, John H. "Portfolio Theory and the Problem of Foreign Exchange Risk." *The Journal of Finance*, 33 (May 1978), 517-534.
This paper introduces an alternative to the usual analysis of ways to deal with the risks involved in open foreign currency positions where exchange rates are uncertain.

Makin, John H. "Portfolio Theory and the Problem of Foreign Exchange Risk: Reply." *The Journal of Finance*, 36 (June 1981), 743-746.
This is a reply by John H. Makin on Daniel Freidman's comments appearing in the same issue.

Mathur, Ike. "Attitudes of Financial Executives Toward Foreign Exchange Issues." *Financial Executive*, 48 (October 1980), 22-26.
This study was designed to look at the attitudes of financial executives toward a variety of foreign exchange issues and to examine the risk management practices of U.S. multinationals.

McEnally, Richard W., and Michael L. Rice. "Hedging Possibilities in the Flotation of Debt Securities." *Financial Management*, 8 (Winter 1979), 12-18.
This paper examines and tests strategies to hedge the interest rate risk faced by corporate borrowers with interest rate futures contracts.

Murenbeeld, Martin. "Economic Factors for Forecasting Foreign Exchange Rate Changes." *Columbia Journal of World Business*, 10 (Summer 1975), 81-95.
This article discusses a discriminant model for judging when currency revaluation/devaluations are likely to occur. Substantial evidence accentuates the value of the model.

Naidu, G.N., and Tai S. Shin. "Effectiveness of Currency Futures Market in Hedging Foreign Exchange Risk." *Management International Review*, 21 (1981, 4), 5-16.
The purposes of this paper are to examine and see how effective the currency futures market has been in hedging, to determine the optimal proportion of exposed spot position that must be hedged in the futures market, and to examine the impact of the basis and its change on the hedger's

profitability.

Neukomm, Hans U. "Risk and Error Minimization in Foreign Exchange Trading." Columbia Journal of World Business, 10 (Winter 1975), 77-85.
The author analyzes foreign exchange operations, and offers a "control" framework aimed at minimizing losses in these high-risk operations.

Oldfield, George S., and Richard J. Messina. "Forward Exchange Price Determination in Continuous Time." Journal of Financial and Quantitative Analysis, 12 (September 1977), 473-479.
This paper uses a continuous time hedging model to derive the interest rate parity theory of foreign exchange as an efficient market equilibrium condition.

Olstein, R.A., and T.L. O'glove. "Devaluation and Multinational Reporting." Financial Analysts Journal, 29 (September/October 1973), 65-69.
The authors point out that approximately 80 of the top 200 U.S. companies generate more than 25 per cent of their sales and earnings from operations abroad. Because of the broad variety of options in the way they account for foreign earnings and assets in dollar terms, the effects of recent dollar devaluations vary from one to another.

Parker, Mark R. "The Numeraire Problem and Foreign Exchange Risk." The Journal of Finance, 36 (May 1981), 419-426, 440-442.
The purpose of this paper is to show that the assumption that home currency is risk free is not generally correct, and to suggest an index that more accurately measures exchange risk.

Reiss, John. "Currency Risk: The Disappearing Profits Trick." Accountancy, 91 (March 1980), 105-106.
This article deals with the potential risks of currency exposure, and the author outlines several ways of avoiding exchange risk.

Robichek, Alexander A., and Mark R. Eaker. "Foreign Exchange Hedging and the Capital Asset Pricing Model." The Journal of Finance, 33 (June 1978), 1011-1018.
The basic proposition advanced and tested empirically in this paper is that a firm's or an individual's foreign exchange position must be analyzed within the context of the capital asset pricing model.

Rodriguez, Rita M. "Management of Foreign Exchange Risk in the U.S. Multinationals." Journal of Financial and Quantitative Analysis, 9 (November 1974), 849-857.
This project is designed to shed light on the management of the size and exchange composition of financial assets and liabilities in U.S. MNCs. The study also intends to analyze the impact of these policies on the international and national financial markets.

Rodriguez, Rita M. "Management of Foreign Exchange Risk in U.S. Multinationals." Sloan Management Review, 19 (Spring 1978), 31-50.
This article focuses on approaches to the management of foreign exchange exposure. Based on a survey of 75 U.S. multinationals, the author concludes that managements have asymmetrical attitudes towards risks in the foreign exchange markets.

Rodriguez, Rita M. "Measuring Multinationals' Exchange Risk." Financial Analysts Journal, 35 (November/December 1978), 49-56.
The author suggests that hedging policies that do not take account of the firm's economic exposure can not only fail to reduce relevant exchange risk, but can actually increase the riskiness of the company by creating exposure where none existed before.

Rodriguez, Rita M. "Corporate Exchange Risk Management: Theme and Aberration." The Journal of Finance, 36 (May 1981), 427-438, 442-444.
This paper summarizes a continuing study involving both extensive and repeated interviews with the chief international financial officers of major U.S. MNCs and the evaluation of financial data regarding the foreign exchange positions of the firms.

Rogalski, Richard J., and Joseph D. Vinso. "Empirical Properties of Foreign Exchange Rates." Journal of International Business Studies, 9 (Fall 1978), 69-79.
The purpose of this paper is to provide some empirical evidence with respect to behavior of foreign exchange rates.

Rossitch, Eugene, and Jack M. Meckler. "Foreign Currency Exposure Control." Management Accounting, 55 (July 1973), 29-37.
To service MNCs, the Wachovia Bank & Trust Company, N.A. developed "Multiplan" for the multinational projection of assets, liabilities, and net worth. The plan is described in this article.

Rueschhoff, Norlin G. "U.S. Dollar Based Financial Reporting of Canadian Multinational Corporations." The International Journal of Accounting Education and Research, 8 (Spring 1973), 103-109.
The author discusses five possible currency bases that may be appropriate for international financial reporting to investors.

Schwab, Bernhard, and Peter Lusztig. "Apportioning Foreign Exchange Risk Through the Use of Third Currencies: Some Questions on Efficiency." Financial Management, 7 (Autumn 1978), 25-30.
This paper explores the question of how international loans should be denominated in order to minimize the total risk to be borne by both borrower and lender.

Serfass, William D., Jr. "You Can't Outguess the Foreign Exchange Market." Harvard Business Review, 54 (March-April 1976), 134-137.
The author describes the program he directs at HMW Industries for the purpose of hedging for exchange risk.

Shapiro, Alan C. "Exchange Rate Changes, Inflation, and the Value of the Multinational Corporation." The Journal of Finance, 30 (May 1975), 485-502.
This paper, with the aid of a two-country model, first focuses on the profitability issue. It then characterizes and analyzes an oligopolistic firm's binational profit-maximizing strategy under inflation and devaluation.

Shapiro, Alan C., and David P. Rutenberg. "Managing Exchange Risks in a Floating World." Financial Management, 5 (Summer 1976), 48-58.
The authors discuss methods of predicting exchange rates and ways accounting exposure can lead one to misconstrue decisions to be made. This article deals with hedging, borrowing, and intracompany maneuvers, and recommends the use of chance-constrained programming to map out the degree of accounting risk that corporate managers choose to bear.

Shapiro, Alan C. "Defining Exchange Risk." The Journal of Business, 50 (January 1977), 37-39.
This article develops a utility-theoretic definition of exposure. Using this definition, an optimal level of exposure in an accounting sense is then found for the MNC.

Sherwin, James T. "Foreign Exchange Exposure Management." Financial Executive, 47 (May 1979), 18-23.
The author expresses the opinion that foreign exchange

exposures present corporate management with very serious problems. He suggests a framework for coping with the continuing uncertainties of foreign exchange.

Soenen, Luc. "Foreign Exchange Exposure Management." Management International Review, 19 (1979/2), 31-38. This article describes the different kinds of foreign exchange exposure and the various strategies and methods of foreign exchange exposure management.

Srinivasulu, S.L. "Strategic Response to Foreign Exchange Risks." Columbia Journal of World Business, 16 (Spring 1981), 13-23. Based on the experience of two MNCs--Volkswagen and Rolls Royce--this paper demonstrates the relevancy of currency risk analysis in strategy formulation.

Stanley, Marjorie, and Stanley Block. "Portfolio Diversification of Foreign Exchange Risk: An Empirical Study." Management International Review, 20 (1980/1), 83-92. This study examines what financial managers are actually doing in the way of foreign exchange portfolio management. It also assesses the organizational structures being employed, the techniques being used for performance measurement, and the financial manager's perception of risk tolerance and time horizon for decision making.

Stokes, Houston H., and Hugh Neuburger. "Interest Arbitrage, Forward Speculation and the Determination of the Forward Exchange Rate." Columbia Journal of World Business, 14 (Winter 1979), 86-98. The authors use the Box-Jenkins time series forecasting technique to test a version of the "modern theory" of forward exchange rates.

Stockton, K.J. "Currency Hedging and Related Problems." The Australian Accountant, 49 (January-February 1979), 33-35. This article describes the official foreign currency market in Australia and how it operates, the unofficial currency hedge market, and gives a working example of a hedge contract.

Teck, Alan. "Control Your Exposure to Foreign Exchange." Harvard Business Review, 52 (January-February 1974), 66-75. The author asserts that the time has come for business to discourage the tendency of governments to endlessly revise and expand regulatory structures for dealing with currency fluctuations.

Upson, Roger B. "Random Walk and Forward Exchange Rates:
A Spectral Analysis." Journal of Financial and Quantitative Analysis, 7 (September 1972), 1897-1905.
This paper examines the random-walk hypothesis in the forward exchange market by applying spectral analysis to the
three-month forward rates for dollars against sterling in
the period 1961-1967.

Walton, Horace C. "Foreign Currency--To Hedge or Not to
Hedge." Financial Executive, 42 (April 1974), 48-55.
The author states that hedging usually involves both a
forecast and an action. He then describes activities that
the financial manager of a MNC has to execute to minimize
company exposure.

Wentz, Rolf-Christian. "Towards a General Foreign Exchange
Risk Consciousness." Columbia Journal of World Business,
14 (Winter 1979), 127-135.
The author outlines some principles for the management of
exchange risk: measuring exposure, forecasting currencies
and hedging.

Wihlborg, Clas. "Economics of Exposure Management of Foreign Subsidiaries of MNCs." Journal of International Business Studies, 11 (Winter 1980), 9-18.
This article represents an extension of a more theoretical
analysis of currency risk. It also develops expressions
for the anticipated dividend payment of a foreign subsidiary
of a multinational corporation.

Political Risk Management

Bradley, David G. "Managing Against Expropriation." Harvard Business Review, 55 (July-August 1977), 75-83.
Drawing on data from Harvard Business School and U.S.
government studies, this article discusses the vulnerability
of MNCs to expropriation and provides help for the international manager to gauge the relative security of his company.

Brewer, Thomas L. "Political Risk Assessment for Foreign
Direct Investment Decisions: Better Methods for Better
Result." Columbia Journal of World Business, 16 (Spring
1981), 5-12.
This article suggests several ways to improve political
risk assessments for foreign direct investment decisions.

Choi, Frederick D.S. "Political Risk--An Accounting

Challenge." Management Accounting, 60 (June 1979), 17-20.
The author points out the threat of expropriation that
haunts MNCs, and illustrates the role that management accountants can play in both forecasting expropriatory actions and minimizing the impact on their corporation.

Jones, Randall J. "A Model For Predicting Expropriation in
Latin America Applied to Jamaica." Columbia Journal of
World Business, 15 (Spring 1980), 74-80.
The author develops a statistical model for predicting
expropriation, and demonstrates that it could have been
used to successfully predict Jamaica's nationalization of
foreign-owned bauxite mining operations.

Kobrin, Stephen J. "When Does Political Instability Result
in Increased Investment Risk?" Columbia Journal of World
Business, 13 (Fall 1978), 113-122.
The author tries to answer the question of how political
conflict in non-industrial countries affects flows of
foreign investment in the manufacturing sector.

McCosker, Joseph S. "Accounting Valuations in Nationalization Settlements." Journal of International Business Studies, 4 (Fall 1973), 15-29.
The purpose of this study is to examine the fairness of
settlements for nationalized properties that are based on
book values and to offer suggestions for accountants in
this connection.

Micallef, Joseph. "Political Risk Assessment." Columbia
Journal of World Business, 16 (Summer 1981), 47-52.
This article suggests that to be effective, a political
risk assessment should first identify those elements of political risk associated with a foreign direct investment
and develop an intelligence system to monitor and evaluate
changing conditions in the host country, integrate the
political risk assessment with the firm's strategic planning, and devise strategies to protect the firm from political risk, especially expropriation.

Rummel, R.J., and David A. Heenan. "How Multinationals
Analyze Political Risk." Harvard Business Review, 56
(January-February 1978), 67-76.
Taking Indonesia as an example, the authors demonstrate an
integrated approach to help executives in evaluating any
foreign investment.

Shapiro, Alan C. "Managing Political Risk: A Policy
Approach." Columbia Journal of World Business, 16 (Fall

1981), 63-70.
Unless a firm continually renews benefits to the host country by introducing more products or by expanding output and developing export markets, it is likely to be subject to increasing political risks.

Van Agtmael, Antoine W. "How Business Has Dealt With Political Risk." Financial Executive, 44 (January 1976), 26-31.
The author explains some of the reasons for nationalization and expropriations, and also summarizes types of political risks and describes a strategy for minimizing this risk.

Control and Performance Evaluation of Foreign Operations

AlHashim, Dhia. "Internal Performance Evaluation in American Multinational Enterprises." Management International Review, 20 (1980/3), 33-39.
The objective of this paper is to deal with the effect of the environmental forces surrounding the operations of U.S.-based MNEs on the selection of the accounting tools used to control and coordinate these operations.

Dietemann, Gerard J. "Evaluating Multinational Performance Under FAS No. 8." Management Accounting, 61 (May 1980), 49-55.
This article examines several alternative methods of presenting foreign earnings in terms meaningful to U.S. management for evaluating multinational performance and then proposes a method that serves this objective best.

Farag, Shawki M. "The Problem of Performance Evaluation in International Accounting." The International Journal of Accounting Education and Research, 10 (Fall 1974), 45-53.
The author states that research on the problem of performance evaluation in international accounting should be approached on two levels that are intrinsically linked. The first is what the most important indicators of the state of the economy in the host country are, and the second is the performance evaluation of the entity.

Garda, J.A. "The Measurement of Financial Data in Evaluating Overseas Managerial Efficiency." The International Journal of Accounting Education and Research, 12 (Fall 1976), 13-18.
The author describes the policies and procedures used by International Harvester in the measurement and evaluation of overseas managerial efficiency of its foreign operations.

Imdieke, Leroy, and Charles Smith. "International Financial Control Problems and the Accounting Control System." Management International Review, 15 (1974/4-5), 13-28. This article identifies and discusses a number of important financial control problems faced by international companies, such problems representing an extension of and not an addition to financial control problems faced by companies having domestic operations only.

Lessard, Donald R., and Peter Lorange. "Currency Changes and Management Control: Resolving the Centralization/Decentralization Dilemma." The Accounting Review, 52 (July 1977), 628-637. This article illustrates the impact of differing treatments of exchange rate changes in budgeting and tracking the performance of decentralized operating units, and concludes with a discussion of how internal forward rates should be set and updated.

Morsicato, Helen G., and Lee H. Radebaugh. "Internal Performance Evaluation of Multinational Enterprise Operations." The International Journal of Accounting Education and Research, 15 (Fall 1979), 77-94. This paper focuses on the interaction of financial statement translation and performance evaluation of foreign operations, primarily from the viewpoint of a U.S.-based MNE, although an extension of the ideas could be made to MNEs domiciled in countries other than the United States.

Morsicato, Helen G., and Michael A. Diamond. "An Approach to 'Environmentalizing' Multinational Enterprise Performance Evaluation Systems." The International Journal of Accounting Education and Research, 16 (Fall 1980), 247-266. This paper integrates the Farmer-Richman Model into the development of performance evaluation standards for the managers of MNEs. The result of this integration makes it possible to systematically incorporate environmental factors into the evaluation of managerial performance.

Motekat, Ula K. "Performance Evaluation in the German Democratic Republic." The Woman CPA, 42 (January 1980), 26-28. This article describes performance evaluation in the German Democratic Republic.

Robbins, Sidney M., and Robert B. Stobaugh. "The Bent Measuring Stick For Foreign Subsidiary." Harvard Business Review, 51 (September-October 1973), 80-88. The authors maintain that MNEs consistently err when they apply companywide measurement standards to foreign subsidiaries. They assess current measurement practices of MNEs, and offer some guidelines for judging subsidiary performance in all its complexities.

Robbins, Sidney M., and Robert B. Stobaugh. "The Profit Potential of Multinational Enterprises." Columbia Journal of World Business, 8 (Fall 1973), 140-153.
The authors point out that the MNE can shuttle funds to take advantage of different tax, money market, and currency relationships throughout the world. Yet extensive interviews revealed that few attempt to integrate those elements into a system to take optimum advantage of them.

Rodney, Earl. "Financial Controls For Multinational Operations." Financial Executive, 44 (May 1976), 26-29.
The author states that financial controls are as good as the people administering them. The key to a successful operation is to have a strong central office controller overseeing the network, and strong local controllers in the various operations.

Scott, George M. "Financial Control in Multinational Enterprises--The New Challenge to Accountants." The International Journal of Accounting Education and Research, 7 (Spring 1972), 55-68.
This article shows that MNEs constitute a different economic phenomenon than has existed before on the world business scene, and informs accountants about the probable impact of MNEs on management and on management information systems, and derivatively on accounting, accountants, and the education of accountants.

Shetty, Y., and Vernon Buehler. "Corporate Responsibility in Large-Scale American Firms: Implications for Multinationals." Management International Review, 16 (1976/1), 25-33.
This exploratory study is designed to determine some of the structural changes taking place in large-scale American companies, to identify the nature and scope of company programs, and to assess company motivations for social actions. Additionally, the authors' analysis discusses the implications of these findings for MNCs.

Sim, A. "Decentralized Management of Subsidiaries and Their Performance: A Comparative Study of American, British, and Japanese Subsidiaries in Malaysia." Management International Review, 17 (1977/3), 45-52.
The purpose of a comparative study of 20 matched American,

British, and Japanese subsidiaries operating in Malaysia
was to determine empirically the pattern and degree of de-
centralization in the subsidiaries, and the relationship
between decentralized management of subsidiaries and their
performance.

Tse, Paul S. "Evaluating Performance in Multinationals."
Management Accounting, 60 (June 1979), 21-25.
The author discusses some of the deficiencies of MNC performance evaluation systems and suggests more realistic alternatives.

Transfer Pricing

Arpan, Jeffrey S. "International Intracorporate Pricing:
Non-American Systems and Views." Journal of International
Business Studies, 3 (Spring 1972), 1-18.
The purpose of this article is to identify similarities and
differences in systems of international intracorporate pri-
cing and to determine the underlying causes.

Arpan, Jeffrey S. "Transfer Pricing in Multinational Financial Management." The Financial Review, 2 (1972), 141-
155.
The focus of this research is on identifying similarities
and differences among non-U.S. firms in terms of the transfer pricing systems they use and the problem areas (both
internal and external) they consider in the design of their
systems. These findings are then compared with those generated by previous research on U.S. multinationals.

Burns, Jane O. "Transfer Pricing Decisions in U.S. Multinational Corporations." Journal of International Business
Studies, 11 (Fall 1980), 23-39.
This paper provides information about the effect 14 variables have on transfer pricing decisions in 62 MNCs. By
means of Student's t-test and -10 level of significance,
it is determined that some variables and factors do have
greater influence on transfer pricing decisions for some
types of companies.

Burns, Jane O., and Ronald S. Ross. "Establishing International Transfer Pricing Standards for Tax Audits of Multinational Enterprises." The International Journal of Accounting Education and Research, 17 (Fall 1981), 161-180.
This paper focuses on the establishment of international
transfer pricing standards for tax audits.

Coburn, David L., Joseph K. Ellis III, and Duane R. Milano. "Dilemmas in MNC Transfer Pricing." Management Accounting, 63 (November 1981), 53-58.
In this article, the authors deal with the reason for various international transfer pricing strategies.

Cowen, Scott S. "Multinational Transfer Pricing." Management Accounting, 60 (January 1979), 17-22.
The author outlines some complications in formulating a transfer pricing system and describes some of the management accounting strategies and resulting tax consequences.

Elam, Rick, and Hamid Henaidy. "Transfer Pricing for the Multinational Corporation." The International Journal of Accounting Education and Research, 16 (Spring 1981), 49-65.
The purpose of this study is to demonstrate the relationship between the problems of transfer pricing and resource allocation and to develop a mathematical model considering the critical environmental aspects which directly affect prices in a profit-maximizing MNC.

Fantl, Irving. "Transfer Pricing--Tread Careful." The CPA Journal, 44 (December 1974), 42-46.
This article examines the problems encountered in setting up transfer prices for the goods and services exchanged between two affiliates with some emphasis on MNCs.

Fowler, D.J. "Transfer Prices and Profit Maximization in Multinational Operations." Journal of International Business Studies, 9 (Winter 1978), 9-26.
This paper shows that the profit maximizing price is a function of the level of ownership in the subsidiary, the dividends payout ratio of the subsidiary, the effective marginal tax rates in both parent and subsidiary countries, and the tariff on the goods transferred.

Kaye, Rodney. "Transfer Pricing." The Accountant, 182 (10 April 1980), 536-538.
Since the various countries through which MNCs operate tax trading profits at different rates of tax, opportunities exist for these MNCs to reduce their world-wide tax liabilities by adjusting the transfer prices in such a way that profits arise in countries with relatively low rates of tax.

Kim, Seung H., and Stephen W. Miller. "Constituents of the International Transfer Pricing Decision." Columbia Journal of World Business, 14 (Spring 1979), 69-77.
The authors establish a theoretical framework for world-

wide transfer pricing with specific reference to developing
countries.

Lamp, Walter. "The Multinational Whipping Boy." Financial
Executive, 44 (December 1976), 44-47.
The author discusses the issue of transfer pricing for multinational enterprises. He gives a brief rundown on some
of the factors that sophisticated multinational companies
are aware of and which generally lead them to steer well
away from the practice of artificial transfer prices.

Malmstom, Duane. "Accommodating Exchange Rate Fluctuations
in Intercompany Pricing and Invoicing." Management Accounting, 59 (September 1977), 24-28.
The purpose of this article is to explain how Honeywell's
Control Systems Organizations solved the problem of pricing
and invoicing intercompany sales among its various subsidiaries and divisions.

Merville, Larry J., and J. William Petty. "Transfer Pricing for the Multinational Firm." The Accounting Review,
53 (October 1978), 935-951.
The purpose of this paper is to consider the transfer pricing mechanism as a powerful tool for achieving conflicting
corporate goals in a world environment. The transfer pricing problem is couched in both a linear programming and a
goal programming framework.

Nagy, Richard J. "Transfer Price Accounting For MNCs."
Management Accounting, 59 (January 1978), 34-38.
The author proposes a system of transfer prices that cap-
tures information in a timely manner so that management
can make decisions concerning any particular activity.

Petty, J. William, and Ernest W. Walker. "Optimal Transfer
Pricing for the Multinational Firm." Financial Management,
1 (Winter 1972), 74-87.
This article explains the role of transfer pricing decisions
within the MNE, builds toward an "optimal" transfer-pricing
concept, and indicates its limitations.

Plasschaert, Sylvain R.F. "The Multiple Motivations for
Transfer Pricing Modulations in Multinational Enterprises
and Governmental Counter-Measures: An Attempt At Clarifi-
cation." Management International Review, 21 (1981/1),
49-63.
This article draws attention to the multiple reasons why
MNEs may be tempted to modulate, to their benefit, the vo-
lumes and the "prices" of payment flows between affiliated

units of the MNE.

Stewart, J.C. "Multinational Companies and Transfer Pricing." Journal of Business Finance & Accounting, 4 (Autumn 1977), 353-371.
The purpose of this paper is to summarize and comment on viewpoints and empirical evidence, in order to identify the key variables which are thought to influence MNCs' financial behavior, focusing particularly on transfer pricing.

Tang, Roger Y.W., C.K. Walter, and Robert H. Raymond. "Transfer Pricing--Japanese vs American Style." Management Accounting, 60 (January 1979), 12-16.
This article reports the result of a research project that was conducted through the use of a questionnaire survey of 300 American and 369 Japanese companies as to methods used by the companies for transfer pricing.

Tang, Roger Y.W., and K.H. Chan. "Environmental Variables of International Transfer Pricing: A Japan-United States Comparison." Abacus, 15 (June 1979), 3-12.
The objectives of this paper are to determine the more important variables considered by large U.S. and Japanese MNCs in formulating their international transfer pricing policies, and to identify the environmental variables which discriminate between the American and Japanese international transfer pricing practices.

Tang, Roger Y.W. "Canadian Transfer Pricing Practices." CA Magazine, 113 (March 1980), 32-38.
This study reports the results of a survey conducted in the Spring and Summer of 1978 of the transfer-pricing policies of 192 Canadian industrial companies.

Wu, Frederick H., and Douglas Sharp. "An Empirical Study of Transfer Pricing Practices." The International Journal of Accounting Education and Research, 14 (Spring 1979), 71-100.
This study seeks to find out what the dominant transfer pricing system is when market prices are available or when market prices are not available, what the motivation criteria are that account for the dominance of some transfer pricing systems, what the dominant arbitration methods are to settle transfer price disputes, and whether there is any difference between domestic and international transfer pricing practices.

International Tax Planning

Arthur, Robert J. "Obtaining Tax Data From Foreign Affiliates." The International Tax Journal, 4 (October 1977), 596-652.
This article discusses some of the information which is needed from foreign organizations and how the tax manager can obtain it.

Bartlett, R.T. "The Taxation of Overseas Earnings." The Accountant, 178 (26 January 1978), 103-106.
The author discusses the Finance Act of 1977 which has brought about some important amendments to 1974 legislation with regard to an office or employment, the duties of which are performed wholly or partly outside the UK.

Bawly, Dan. "The Multinational Company." Accountancy, 84 (December 1973), 80-86.
This is the first of a two-part article on the taxation problems of MNCs, and deals with tax havens.

Bawly, Dan. "The Multinational Company--II." Accountancy, 85 (January 1974), 69-71.
In the second of a two-part article on taxation problems of MNCs, the author highlights government incentives for MNCs.

Berg, Robert. "The Effect of the New UK/US Double Tax Treaty." Accountancy, 88 (November 1977), 70-71.
This article highlights the principal amendments of the 1975 UK/US Tax Treaty to the original Treaty of 1945.

Binkowski, Edward. "Tax Consequences of Creeping Expropriation." The International Tax Journal, 7 (December 1980), 117-126.
This article describes current issues concerning gradual expropriation.

Brantner, Paul F. "Taxation and the Multinational Firm." Management Accounting, 55 (October 1973), 11-16.
This article analyzes the United States tax system, how the tax system has changed to cope with the MNC, and how the MNC has carried the influence of the U.S. tax system to other countries.

Briner, Ernst K. "International Tax Management." Management Accounting, 54 (February 1973), 47-50.
International corporations face special tax problems in terms of United States taxes and the taxes of other countries. An insight into some of these problems is offered

in this article.

Broke, Adam. "How are Foreign Earnings Taxed?" Accountancy, 87 (May 1976), 68-70.
This article provides an updated guide to the complexities
of tax liability on foreign earnings in the UK.

Burns, Jane O. "Exports and the Tax Reform Act of 1976."
The International Tax Journal, 4 (February 1978), 810-823.
This article examines and compares the federal income tax
advantages of the WHTC and the DISC as modified by the Tax
Reform Act of 1976.

Burns, Jane O. "DISC Accounting: An Empirical Investigation." The International Tax Journal, 4 (April 1978),
882-891.
This article reports the results of a questionnaire survey
of companies as to how they operate their DISCs and record
financial data relevant to their DISCs. The responses are
divided into four topic areas where the DISC legislation
causes recording problems for accountants: the separate
corporate shares of the DISC; the deferral as temporary or
permanent; intercompany pricing; and the DISC assets test.

Burns, Jane O. "Professors' Foreign Travel Expenses: Deductible or Nondeductible?" The Accounting Review, 53
(July 1978), 736-745.
This article examines federal income tax legislation and
pertinent court cases relating to foreign travel, to enable
the professor and his family to guard against loss of significant tax deductions when travelling abroad.

Burns, Jane O. "How IRS Applies the Intercompany Pricing
Rules of Section 482: A Corporate Survey." The Journal of
Taxation, 52 (May 1980), 308-314.
This study reports the experiences of 62 corporations with
Section 482 audits, focusing on transfer pricing methods,
the audit itself, IRS administration, and suggestions for
change.

Burns, Jane O. "Taxation Policies for Plant and Equipment
In Industrial Nations." The Tax Executive, 34 (October
1981), 1-10.
The author outlines taxation policies for plant and equip-
ment in Canada, France, West Germany, Japan, the United
Kingdom, and the United States.

Calhoun, Donald A. "The Foreign Tax Credit." Management
Accounting, 57 (September 1975), 41-42, 53.

The author of this article explains the importance of creating tax incentives for American companies to do business outside the U.S. He also explains the provision of the tax law that allows MNEs foreign tax credit, and the methods of computing this tax credit.

Calitri, Joseph C. "The Challenge of Burke-Hartke." Financial Executive, 40 (June 1972), 36-39.
The author summarizes issues leading to the Burke-Hartke bill, and exhorts MNCs to make known to the American public the vital role these companies serve in our economy.

Carmichael, Keith. "Tax on Foreign Earnings." Accountancy, 85 (October 1974), 84-86.
The author provides details on Britain's 1974 Finance Act, which changed the tax position on foreign earnings.

Carmichael, Keith. "Tax on Foreign Earnings." Accountancy, 88 (June 1977), 46-52.
The author details the provisions of the Finance Bill 1977 concerning foreign earnings.

Chan, K.H., and Herbert L. Jensen. "Tax Accounting for Capital Assets--The US vs. Canada." CA Magazine, 112 (December 1979), 36-41.
This article examines the major differences in the way Canada and the US deal with depreciation deductions and tax credits, both to clarify the laws and to make it easier to take advantage of the various possible tax savings.

Choate, Alan G., and Michael L. Moore. "Bribes and Boycotts Under the Tax Reform Act of 1976." The International Tax Journal, 4 (December 1977), 736-744.
This article discusses the new concepts and consequences of the payment of bribes or participation in boycotts under the Tax Reform Act of 1976.

Chown, John. "Towards Tax Unifications." Accountancy, 83 (June 1972), 23-25.
The author discusses broadly the varied methods of taxing companies and shareholders in the EEC member countries.

Christie, Andrew J. "The UK/Norway Double Tax Treaty." The Accountant's Magazine, 83 (December 1979), 514-515.
The author examines the effects of a Protocol on the UK/ Norway Tax Treaty and asks whether the provisions of the Protocol could be the shape of things to come as far as double tax treaties with other oil-producing countries are concerned.

Cretton, Colin, and Alan Reid. "A Practitioner's Guide to the UK/US Double Tax Treaty (Part 1)." Accountancy, 91 (June 1980), 101-102.
This is the first of a series of three articles, the purpose of which is to outline and comment upon some of the provisions of the UK/US double taxation convention ratified by Parliament on 18 February 1980 which entered into force on 25 April 1980. In this article the scope of the treaty is outlined, and the position of the UK resident doing business in the US is considered.

Cretton, Colin, and Alan Reid. "A Practitioner's Guide to the UK/US Double Tax Treaty (Part 2)." Accountancy, 91 (August 1980), 52-53.
The authors look at the effects of the UK/US double tax treaty on investment income and earnings from personal activities, and discuss the machinery for giving double tax relief where a UK resident's income is taxable in the US.

Cretton, Colin, and Alan Reid. "A Practitioner's Guide to the UK/US Double Tax Treaty (Part 3)." Accountancy, 91 (October 1980), 97-98.
In this final article in the series, the treaty provisions are considered from the standpoint of the US resident with income or gains arising in the UK.

Davis, Michael. "The Tax Haven Company--Dispelling the Myths." Accountancy, 87 (February 1976), 46-48.
The author points out the substantial hindrances that face the UK resident who wants to operate through a tax haven company. He discusses the UK Sections 478 and 482 of the Income and Corporation Taxes Act.

Deakin, B. "Country by Country Aspects of VAT." Accountancy, 83 (February 1972), 76-79.
This article is concerned with various aspects of the value added tax as they apply in Britain and other EEC countries. The author defines the problems of this complex tax and outlines the interim stages of application.

Delap, Richard L. "Apportionment of Expenses to DISC Income." The International Tax Journal, 5 (February 1979), 214-226.
The author states that those deductions of greatest relevance to the determination of combined taxable income of a DISC are not considered in the regulation, and illustrates some of these deductions.

Dilley, Steven. "Allocation and Apportionment Under

Reg. 1.861.8." The CPA Journal, 50 (December 1980), 33-38.
The author presents a schedule of the information requirements necessary to comply with regulations for allocation
of deductible expenses between foreign and domestic
sources, and offers suggestions on how certain data may be
presented.

Dreier, Ronald. "U.S. Income Tax Treaties." Columbia
Journal of World Business, 10 (Summer 1975), 21-28.
Anyone involved with foreign business should be familiar
with U.S. income tax treaties. Proper structure of foreign
operations utilizing income tax treaties can result in substantial tax savings.

Feinschreiber, Robert. "Tax Benefits for Domestic International Sales Corporations (DISCs)--How to Qualify." The
CPA Journal, 42 (February 1972), 131-138.
This first of a two-part article explores the requirements
for forming and using a Domestic International Sales Corporation.

Feinschreiber, Robert. "Tax Benefits for Domestic International Sales Corporations (DISCs)--Pricing, Profits, and
Dividends." The CPA Journal, 42 (March 1972), 221-224.
This article is the second of two parts; the first appeared in the February 1972 issue of The CPA Journal. This
second part deals with the benefits to be derived from
using a DISC for export sales.

Feinschreiber, Robert. "DISC: A New Export Tax Incentive."
Financial Executive, 40 (April 1972), 66-70.
The author describes how the DISC operates and how a company can take advantage of the tax savings offered by the
statute.

Feinschreiber, Robert. "New Strategies For Increasing DISC
Benefits." Financial Executive, 44 (August 1976), 32-37.
The author states that DISC is producing substantial tax
savings for American business while increasing U.S. exports
at the same time. Thousands of companies are using DISCs
to save hundreds of millions of tax dollars annually, but
there are opportunities for yet greater benefits. The
author states some of these opportunities.

Feinschreiber, Robert. "Allocation and Apportionment of
Miscellaneous Deductions." The International Tax Journal,
4 (October 1977), 653-668.
This article examines the allocation and apportionment of
deductions specifically enumerated in the regulations

pertaining to legal and accounting fees and expense, state
and foreign income taxes, losses on property dispositions,
net operating losses, and special deductions.

Feinschreiber, Robert. "Allocation and Apportionment of
Research Expenses." The International Tax Journal, 4
(April 1978), 902-924.
A special rule permits research to be apportioned to a
specific geographic source if the research is undertaken
solely to meet legal requirements imposed by that geographic source. Here, the author turns his attention first to
the general allocation approach, and then to the special
"legal requirements" allocation method.

Feinschreiber, Robert. "Treaty Provisions for Allocating
and Apportioning Deductions." The International Tax Journal, 4 (June 1978), 995-1006.
This article examines the general facets of deduction apportionment, analyzes the apportionment rules in treaties
to which the U.S. is a party, and compares these rules with
the rules in non-U.S. treaties.

Feinschreiber, Robert. "Analysis of the Allocation and Apportionment Examples." The International Tax Journal, 4
(August 1978), 1027-1070.
The allocation and apportionment regulations contain a number of examples, many of which are both lengthy and complex.
There are 26 examples; this article provides an in-depth
analysis of the first 16, the majority of which pertain to
research expenses. The remaining 10 examples will be analyzed in the next issue of this journal.

Feinschreiber, Robert. "Analysis of the Allocation and Apportionment Examples--Part II." The International Tax
Journal, 5 (October 1978), 45-72.
In the August 1978 issue of The International Tax Journal,
the author began an analysis of the examples contained in
the final regulation for the allocation and apportionment
of deductions. This article contains an analysis of the
final ten examples and considers other expenses, such as
stewardship, supportive expenses, and state income taxes.

Feinschreiber, Robert. "New Deductions for Overseas Americans." The International Tax Journal, 5 (December 1978),
93-108.
This article focuses on explaining the most important of
the various tax benefits available to Americans who live
and work in foreign countries.

Feinschreiber, Robert. "FBC Sales Income and Its Exclusions." The International Tax Journal, 5 (February 1979), 231-250.
This article examines the basic rules for FBC sales income, the exclusion of various types of property, the exclusion for property manufactured in the country in which the CFC is incorporated, the exclusion for property sold in the country in which the CFC is incorporated, and the exclusion for property manufactured by CFC.

Feinschreiber, Robert. "Earnings and Profits Translation of Specific Items." The International Tax Journal, 5 (April 1979), 334-346.
The determination of earnings and profits under Section 964 requires the income statement and the balance sheet to be translated into U.S. dollars. This article examines the problems and opportunities that arise from the translation of specific items.

Feinschreiber, Robert. "Interest-Free International Loans." The International Tax Journal, 5 (June 1979), 394-409.
Interest-free loans between affiliated corporations may no longer be permissible between domestic affiliates, but it is possible that interest-loans can still be made to foreign subsidiaries in some situations. This article examines the cases concerning interest-free loans and then considers the impact of these decisions on international loans between affiliates.

Feinschreiber, Robert. "The Foreign Tax Credit Under Siege." Financial Executive, 47 (October 1979), 56-63.
The author states that recent limitations on foreign tax credits are having an adverse effect on international corporations. However, he proposes that with intelligent planning, multinationals may still be able to obtain the full benefits of the credit.

Feinschreiber, Robert. "Intercompany Pricing After DuPont." The International Tax Journal, 6 (February 1980), 222-229.
This article describes the impact of the Court of Claims ruling for DuPont on intercompany pricing.

Feinschreiber, Robert. "Consolidated Foreign Tax Credit: Analysis of the ITT Case." The International Tax Journal, 6 (April 1980), 302-306.
The issue in ITT was the sequence of two computations, the apportionment of deductions and the aggregation of income. The author provides an analysis of the case.

Feinschreiber, Robert. "How to Double DISC Benefits Through FISC and Grouping." The International Tax Journal, 6 (June 1980), 367-372.
The author tells how it was possible to more than double DISC benefits for one company by establishing a FISC subsidiary and grouping DISC sales in an advantageous manner.

Feinschreiber, Robert. "Apportioning Interest Expense to the U.S. Branch of a Foreign Corporation." The International Tax Journal, 7 (October 1980), 51-75.
This article examines the technical features of a proposed regulation that would modify the fungibility of money concept to include liabilities as well as assets in the computation, and suggests planning strategies for maximizing the interest apportionment for the U.S. business.

Feinschreiber, Robert, and Caryl Nackenson. "Obtaining Interest and Royalties from Foreign Subsidiaries: The Impact of Xerox v. Maryland." The International Tax Journal, 7 (October 1980), 5-13.
This article examines the foreign tax credit strategy utilizing interest and royalty payments from foreign subsidiaries, the court's holding in Xerox v. Maryland, and the adverse tax consequences of their decision on multinational corporations with potential excess foreign tax credits.

Feinschreiber, Robert. "The Impact of Arrow Fastener on DISC Operations." The International Tax Journal, 7 (August 1981), 413-427.
The recent Tax Court decision in Arrow Fastener Co., Inc. has limited the power of the IRS to promulgate DISC regulations that go beyond the statute to the detriment of the taxpayer. This article examines the opinion and its impact on maintaining DISC eligibility.

Finney, Malcolm J. "Taxation and International Financing." The Accountant, 178 (29 June 1978), 882-884.
This article explains some of the more familiar concepts often involved in taxation and international financing.

Gaskins, J. Peter. "Taxation of Foreign Source Income." Financial Analysts Journal, 29 (September/October 1973), 55-64.
The author points out that both foreign and U.S. taxes on foreign source income are likely to increase in the future. The increases should be gradual, however, and even while effective rates of taxation are rising, many MNCs will find new ways to take advantage of existing tax havens.

Green, Alex. "The New UK/Canada Tax Treaty." Accountancy, 90 (August 1979), 83-86.
This article outlines some of the changes introduced by the 1978 New UK/Canada Tax Treaty that replaced the old agreement which was signed in Ottawa in 1966.

Green, Jeffrey. "Foreign Source Income and Dutch Corporate Taxation." The Accountant, 176 (22 June 1977), 635-636.
The Netherlands takes a robust and an unusual view about international double taxation and this, linked with the many double tax treaties which the Netherlands has negotiated with other countries, effectively results in income from non-Netherlands sources being taxed at relatively modest rates.

Green, William H. "Analysis of the 1977 DISC Report." The International Tax Journal, 4 (October 1977), 579-595.
This article examines the data on DISC that was released by the Treasury Department in April 1977 as part of the 1975 Annual Report. It pertains to taxable years ending between July 1, 1974 and June 30, 1975.

Green, William H. "Planning DISC Operations in the '80's." The International Tax Journal, 6 (June 1980), 373-389.
This article first describes some of the highlights and trends indicated by the data in the April 1980 Treasury Report on DISC. Strategies for managing DISC operations and potential problem areas are then considered.

Green, William H. "Analysis of the 1981 Treasury Report On DISC." The International Tax Journal, 7 (June 1981), 333-352.
This article examines the operational data contained in the 1981 Treasury Report on DISC operations. After a review of prior Reports, the data is analyzed for planning present and future DISC activities. Proposals for revising the DISC report and statute also are considered.

Green, William H. "Analysis of the New ITT Case." The International Tax Journal, 7 (August 1981), 466-473.
In his comment on the recent ITT case, the author discusses consolidated foreign tax credit planning and the impact of intercompany charges on apportionment of expenses.

Hammer, Richard. "Financial Planning To Avoid Tax Problems." The International Journal of Accounting Education and Research, 7 (Spring 1972), 23-34.
This paper discusses form of organization as vehicle through which to operate a business abroad, and the tax opportu-

nities available to corporate taxpayers by taking advantage of the Western Hemisphere Trade Corporation and possessions corporate provisions, some of the tax problems arising out of Section 482, and U.S. foreign tax credit rules.

Harless, Donald S. "Recent Rulings Affect Allocation and Apportionment." The International Tax Journal, 7 (August 1981), 461-465.
The author analyzes apportionment of interest and franchise tax expenses and the IRS consistency requirements.

Heinz, Peter Danser. "Mathematical Strategies for the Foreign Tax Credit Limitation." The International Tax Journal, 7 (August 1981), 454-460.
This article presents a mathematical strategy for foreign tax credit planning. The strategy optimizes the limitation formula, based on foreign income, effective tax rates, gross-up, withholding taxes, and other important factors.

Howard, Fred. "Overview of International Taxation." Columbia Journal of World Business, 10 (Summer 1975), 5-11.
This article describes the principal issues and challenges facing businessmen, tax practitioners and government officials in the field of international taxation for the near future.

Hughes, Anthony. "Tax Concessions Ahead in UK/India Treaty." Accountancy, 92 (November 1981), 148-150.
This article deals with a forthcoming UK/India tax treaty. Particular attention has been concentrated on the effects it will have for a UK resident who has, or may have, business dealings with India.

Ioannides, J.D. "Invest in Cyprus: Taxation and Other Incentives." The Accountant, 179 (20 July 1978), 70-71.
The author puts forth many reasons why Cyprus provides an attractive environment for the investor.

James, George F. "MNCs and the Foreign Tax Credit." Columbia Journal of World Business, 9 (Winter 1974), 61-66.
Limitations on or denial of foreign tax credits are now (1974) being proposed by several bills before the U.S. Congress. The author assesses the probable impact of these actions on U.S. foreign investments with an emphasis on the U.S. oil industry.

Kolmin, Frank W., and Christopher W. Nobes. "The Accumulated Earnings Tax: An Anglo-American Comparison." The International Tax Journal, 5 (June 1979), 410-419.

The authors examine the provisions of the British corporate tax laws that pertain to excess corporate accumulated earnings, compare the British provisions with the U.S. rules, and make recommendations for restructuring the U.S. accumulated earning tax.

Lagae, Jean-Pierre, and Patrick Kelley. "Tax Aspects of American Investment In Belgium." The International Tax Journal, 5 (October 1978), 23-34.
The authors consider the tax aspects of the choice between doing business as a subsidiary or as a branch, analyze the tax consequences of the provision of capital, technology, and services to the Belgian operation, and explore the impact of Belgian and U.S. income taxation on U.S. expatriate employees.

Lamp, Walter. "US-UK Tax Treaty Proposal: New Look At Dividends." Financial Executive, 44 (March 1976), 14-25.
This article is aimed at highlighting some of the features of the dividend provisions of the US-UK tax treaty. It includes also an explanation of US foreign tax credit.

Lillie, Jane. "A New Strategy for Recognizing Exchange Gains and Losses." The International Tax Journal, 4 (August 1978), 1071-1080.
This article distinguishes between realized and unrealized and between recognized and unrecognized currency exchange gains and losses of CFCs and considers the determination of currency exchange gains and losses in U.S. dollars, the realization and recognition of these gains and losses for U.S. income tax purposes, and the translation into U.S. dollars of dividends measured in foreign currency.

McDermott, John E., and Martin Oliver. "The Effect of Foreign Source Capital Losses on the Foreign Tax Credit." The International Tax Journal, 4 (December 1977), 679-687.
One major area affected by the Tax Reform Act of 1976 is the foreign tax credit. The authors describe the impact of the Tax Reform Act of 1976 on the foreign tax credit.

Morgan, John R., and Colin Robinson. "The Comparative Effects of the UK and Norwegian Oil Taxation Systems on Profitability and Government Revenue." Accounting and Business Research, 7 (Winter 1976), 2-16.
This article contains a brief review of the tax legislation in the UK and Norway, compares the two systems quantitatively, and examines their relative performance under a wide range of key assumptions.

Ness, Walter L. "U.S. Corporate Income Taxation and the Dividend Remission Policy of Multinational Corporations." Journal of International Business Studies, 6 (Spring 1975), 67-78.
This article indicates that features of the U.S. taxation of the income of MNCs is shown to affect the minimum rate of return required on the unremitted profits of foreign subsidiaries. It also develops criteria that should be used by the firm as the minimum required return on reinvested earnings as the result of various fiscal devices.

Newman, Barry, and Jefferey Kadet. "United States Taxation of Foreign Flag Shipping." Columbia Journal of World Business, 12 (Spring 1977), 103-111.
In the past, United States tax treatment of foreign-flag shipping companies as well as other business considerations have encouraged the formation of foreign corporations to hold United States controlled ships. However, recent changes and discussion of possible future modification of the tax law indicate a trend by United States' authorities to limit the advantages of foreign operations.

Nobes, Christopher. "Corporation Tax: Toward EEC Harmonization." Accountancy, 90 (January 1979), 52-55.
This article outlines the systems of corporate taxation in operation in the three EEC countries of greatest importance to the UK for trading and investment: France, West Germany and the Netherlands.

Nobes, C.W. "Imputation System of Corporation Tax Within the EEC." Accounting and Business Research, 10 (Spring 1980), 221-231.
This article contrasts the working of imputation in the UK and other countries, examines one of the Meade Committee's proposals for reform, discusses the behavior of the UK system during an inflationary period, and looks at the purposes and current progress of harmonization of corporate taxation in the EEC.

Nordhauser, Susan L., and John L. Kramer. "Repeal of the Deferral Privilege for Earnings from Direct Foreign Investments: An Analysis." The Accounting Review, 56 (January 1981), 54-69.
This paper examines the likelihood that U.S.-based MNEs will alter their corporate structure in response to changes in U.S. tax policies toward income derived from direct foreign investments.

O'Connor, Walter F., and Samuel M. Russo. "Tax Consequences

of the Currency Float." Financial Executive, 43 (January 1975), 48-53.
The authors highlight some of the more common tax problems encountered in conducting international business. More specifically, the tax treatment of foreign currency gains and losses is covered.

Oliver, David. "How Not to Lose Out on the UK/US Tax Treaty." Accountancy, 91 (July 1980), 80-81.
This article is concerned with the new US/UK capital taxes treaty of 1979. The author outlines how certain provisions will apply, and points out that special care is needed where there are financial interests in both countries.

Peckron, Harold S. "Tax Consequences of Currency Futures After Hoover." The International Tax Journal, 6 (February 1980), 165-177.
This article summarizes the decision made that held that forward contracts for the sale of foreign currency gave rise to capital gain or loss rather than to ordinary income or an ordinary deduction.

Perlstein, Pinkus. "International Tax Planning." Accountancy, 87 (December 1976), 69-70.
The author explores the practical value of tax havens, and considers the best method of conducting international operations from a fiscal point of view.

Rädler, Albert J. "International Capital Markets and Taxation." Management International Review, 13 (1973/6), 65-74.
Generally it might be said that the impact of international differentials in direct tax levels is more in the long-run than in the short-run. This paper discusses the influence of taxation on international investments.

Raskhin, Michael D. "The Branch Rule and the Subpart F Exclusion." The International Tax Journal, 4 (June 1978), 980-994.
This article first considers the two Subpart F exceptions, and then examines the branch rule.

Ravenscroft, Donald R. "Translating Foreign Currency Under U.S. Tax Law." Financial Executive, 42 (September 1974), 58-69.
This article describes the methods of foreign currency translation acceptable under present tax laws, and points out choices available to U.S. taxpayers engaged in international trade to minimize taxes on their investments.

Ravenscroft, Donald R. "Foreign Investment, Exchange Rates, Taxable Income and Real Values." Columbia Journal of World Business, 10 (Summer 1975), 50-61.
This article develops the premise that the nominal dollar equivalent of assets does not coincide with their real value in the host country. Changes in tax laws are suggested to reflect the purchasing power of foreign assets both if used locally and if repatriated to the United States.

Romito, Edwin L. "Amending the DISC Return." The International Tax Journal, 7 (April 1981), 300-308.
The author reviews the current IRS position on amending DISC returns and predicts what its future position could be.

Ryan, Edward D. "International Tax Problems and the Financial Officer." Management Accounting, 57 (October 1975), 49-58.
This article touches upon some of the current tax laws affecting the international corporation. The author expresses his belief that solutions to problems in this area can be resolved through greater awareness by financial officers.

Sale, J. Timothy, and Karen B. Carroll. "Tax Planning Tools for the Multinational Corporation." Management Accounting, 60 (June 1979), 37-41.
This article outlines some of the tax provisions that enable MNCs to reduce their tax liabilities. It includes a description of how MNCs are taxed, advantage of tax treaties and tax havens, and illustrates the foreign tax credit.

Schlag, Rene C. "Accounting for Taxes of Foreign Subsidiaries--A Simplified Approach." Management Accounting, 61 (December 1979), 15-19.
This article presents a condensed approach for calculating taxes on the earnings of foreign subsidiaries and affiliates, together with an explanation of the more important tax concepts involved.

Schmitz, Marvin N. "Taxation of Foreign Exchange Gains and Losses." Management Accounting, 57 (July 1976), 49-51.
The author points out that U.S. tax legislation and IRS rulings in the area of foreign exchange have failed to keep pace with the rapid expansion of international transactions by American business, and offers some guidelines based on Tax Court decisions and IRS rulings.

Schwartz, Bill. "Partial Income Tax Allocation and Deferred Taxation: An International Accounting Issue." Management International Review, 20 (1980/4), 74-82.

This paper defines partial income tax allocation, explains the steps used in the process, and illustrates how partial income tax allocation is applied. Emphasis is given to the provisions of IAS No. 12 and SSAP No. 15.

Seghers, Paul D. "Intercompany Pricing-Tax Audits." The International Tax Journal, 5 (August 1979), 437-441.
IRS examinations that could result in additional U.S. income tax based on Section 482 adjustments of intercompany sales and what to do about them are considered in this article.

Shagam, Jerome, and Kenneth G. Kolmin. "Temporary Regulations Resolve Some Problems for U.S. Persons Working Abroad." The International Tax Journal, 5 (June 1979), 363-393.
This article considers regulations of the Foreign Earned Income Act of 1978 and the Revenue Act of 1978 that significantly affect the taxation of U.S. citizens and resident aliens who live and work abroad.

Simms, Charles A. "Summarizing the Foreign Earned Income Tax Act of 1978." Management Accounting, 61 (August 1979), 32-36.
The author explains the provisions of the Foreign Earned Income Act of 1978 which completely changes the way in which employees (expatriates in foreign services) are to be taxed by the United States.

Simon, Stuart H. "Depreciation Proposal Would Impair Foreign Tax Credit." The International Tax Journal, 7 (June 1981), 353-356.
This article examines the impact of the current Administration's tax proposals on U.S. multinationals. Accelerated capital cost recovery rules can adversely affect foreign tax credit computations.

Smith, C.W. Davidson. "The New United States Double Taxation Agreement." The Accountant's Magazine, 80 (March 1976), 96-97.
This article outlines the more unusual features of the new US/UK tax agreement signed on December 31, 1975.

Stitt, Carl. "The UK as a Tax Haven." The Accountant, 182 (20 March 1980), 436-438.
The establishment of the fiscal residence of a company is often of prime importance in determining the tax jurisdiction of a particular country over a company. This article deals with UK regulations.

Stobaugh, Robert B. "More Taxes On Multinationals."
Financial Executive, 42 (April 1974), 12-17.
This article is based on Professor Stobaugh's testimony
before the House Ways and Means Committee on June 11, 1973,
and a study he directed to evaluate the effect of U.S.
taxation of multinational corporations on the economy.

Symonds, Edward. "Still Hotter Rivalry Under New Tax
Treaty." The Accountant, 182 (10 April 1980), 542-543.
The author discusses changes that will take place with the
implementation of the new UK/US tax treaty.

Tomsett, Eric. "Double Taxation: The New Treaty Between
UK and the Netherlands." Accountancy, 92 (July 1981), 88-
90.
The new double taxation treaty concluded between the Netherlands and the UK has substantially altered the tax position
of Netherland companies in relation to UK investment. The
author of this article examines the significance of the new
treaty and highlights the problems it will create.

Van Valkenburg, Marilyn. "Foreign Income and the Internal
Revenue Code." Management Accounting, 55 (June 1974), 18-
22.
Persons and corporations that earn their income in part or
wholly from foreign operations must abide by specific tax
regulations. Some of those regulations and their effect on
the taxpayer are discussed in this article.

Wainman, David. "Currency Fluctuation: Accounting and
Taxation Implications." The Accountant, 174 (19 August
1976), 211-212.
This article is an excerpt from a book of the same title
by the same author. Several incidents are used to illustrate implications for accounting and taxation.

Yost, George J. "Establishing Intercompany Pricing Com-
parables After U.S. Steel." The International Tax Journal,
6 (June 1980), 360-366.
The final resolution of every intercompany dispute necessarily involves an examination of the specific facts of
each taxpayer's circumstances. The U.S. Steel case provides a certain degree of guidance as to the specifics of
how a taxpayer might establish comparability.

Yost, George J. "Impact of the Debt-Equity Regulations on
International Operations." The International Tax Journal,
7 (February 1981), 217-228.
This article presents a broad overview of new regulations

providing standards to characterize investments as stock or debt. The regulations apply primarily to domestic transactions, but they have a significant impact on international operations.

Yost, George J. "Unwritten International Loans." The International Tax Journal, 7 (April 1981), 253-261.
This article focuses on the recently adopted debt/equity regulations under Section 385. In particular, the author examines the circumstances under which loans may be recharacterized as contributions to capital.

ACCOUNTING STANDARDS AND PRACTICES IN
VARIOUS COUNTRIES

Asia

Barrett, M. Edgar, Lee N. Price, and Judith Ann Gehrke.
"Japan: Some Background for Security Analysts." Financial
Analysts Journal, 30 (January/February 1974), 33-44.
This article deals with two facets of the Japanese economic scene that present significant stumbling blocks to
fundamental analysts: sources of funds for industry, and
financial reporting and analysis.

Barrett, M. Edgar, Lee N. Price, and Judith Ann Gehrke.
"Japan: Some Background for Security Analysts." Financial
Analysts Journal, 30 (March/April 1974), 60-67.
This article is the second part of an article with the same
title that was published in the January/February issue of
Financial Analysts Journal that deals with financial repor-
ting practices in Japan.

Baxter, William T. "Accounting in Japan." The Accountant's Magazine, 80 (November 1976), 433-434.
The author outlines how the accountancy profession in Japan in the 1970s is organized in public practice, auditing,
tax accounting, and in industry.

Bose, Mihir. "The Growth of Accountancy in India." Accountancy, 88 (May 1977), 36-38.
The author contrasts the world of accounting in India with
that of the UK.

Cheng, Philip C., and Tribhowan N. Jain. "Economic Perspective and Accounting Practices in South Korea." The
International Journal of Accounting Education and Research,
8 (Spring 1973), 123-139.
This article discusses economic activity in South Korea
with emphasis on all aspects of accounting. The characteristics of the economic and social environment of the
modern accounting profession in South Korea are discussed,
and an investigation of foreign investment opportunities
follows with some fax features given special attention.

Chiu, James S., and Davis L. Chang. "Management Accounting
in Taiwan." Management Accounting, 60 (June 1979), 50-55.
This article addresses the following questions: Can American management accounting techniques be transferred successfully to other settings? In particular, can they be successfully used in the manufacturing companies of a develo-

ping country such as Taiwan?

Choi, Frederick D.S. "Asean Federation of Accountants: A New International Accounting Force." The International Journal of Accounting Education and Research, 15 (Fall 1979), 53-75.
This paper examines the emerging phenomenon of ASEAN accounting cooperation and its nature, purpose, problems and functional organization, especially with respect to the promulgation of regional accounting standards in Southease Asia.

Dale, Basil. "Accounting in Japan." The Australian Accountant, 49 (April 1979), 150-157.
The author describes the historical development of financial reporting in Japan with more emphasis on the development since World War II, the legal background of financial reporting, auditing and management accounting.

Deakin, Edward B., Gyles R. Norwood, and Charles H. Smith. "The Effect of Published Information on Tokyo Stock Exchange Trading." The International Journal of Accounting Education and Research, 10 (Fall 1974), 123-136.
This study examines both the price and volume reactions of securities traded on the Tokyo Stock Exchange to the release of tax administration information. A supplementary test is also made based on the data generated by the first test.

DuBois, Donald A., and Kyojiro Someya. "Accounting Development in Japan." The Accountant, 176 (5 May 1977), 500-504.
Industrial development, it has been suggested, tends to follow a common pattern irrespective of traditional national or cultural factors. The authors examine this theory in its application to Western Influence—particularly that of the United States—on the Japanese accountancy profession.

Fujita, Yukio. "Japan: Expansion of the Auditors' Function." The Accountant's Magazine, 78 (March 1974), 92-93.
The purpose of this article is to introduce to readers an outline of the proposed revision of the auditing system for stock corporations.

Katsuyama, Susumu. "Recent Problems of Financial Accounting System in Japan." The International Journal of Accounting Education and Research, 12 (Fall 1976), 121-132.
This article discusses the problems of financial accounting systems in Japan, with special reference to international accounting. More specifically, it includes the accounting for foreign currency translation, reevaluation of assets and consolidation principles.

Kohlhagen, Steven W. "Host Country Policies and MNCs--The Pattern of Foreign Investment in Southeast Asia." Columbia Journal of World Business, 12 (Spring 1977), 49-58.
Using the ASEAN countries (Indonesia, Malaysia, the Phillipines, Singapore, and Thailand) as an example, the author examines the circumstances under which current investment patterns have developed and how different policies might generate other patterns in the future.

Kubota, Keiichi. "Information Content of Accounting Numbers: Evidence on Tokyo Stock Exchange Firms." The International Journal of Accounting Education and Research, 15 (Spring 1980), 61-76.
This paper hypothesizes that accounting numbers published in Japan convey information on security returns. Empirical tests are conducted to determine the accuracy of this assertion.

Monroe, Wilbur F. "Exchange Controls in Japan." Financial Analysts Journal, 28 (November/December 1972), 43-48.
The author points out that in early 1971 the yen was widely regarded as one of the strongest of all currencies and a candidate for early revaluation. The Japanese, who wanted to stem any capital inflow before they could upset domestic financial policies dramatize their balance of payment surplus, resorted to capital controls.

Ohno, Nimiyoshi, Hideo Ichikawa, and Atsuyoshi Kodama. "Recent Changes In Accounting Standards in Japan." The International Journal of Accounting Education and Research, 11 (Fall 1975), 107-120.
The authors discuss the following problems focusing on the 1974 amendment of the Statement of Business Accounting Principles: the background which required the reconciliation between the BAPs and the commercial code; the change of the accounting method for allowances which had important consequences for a balance sheet disclosure; and the change in the form of financial statements, especially the income statement.

Ozawa, Terutomo. "Multinationalism--Japanese Style." Columbia Journal of World Business, 7 (November/December 1972), 33-42.
The author discusses Japan's multinationalism, which is complementary to its domestic and industrial transformation. This article is based in part on a report commissioned by the World Bank.

Perera, M.H.B. "Accounting and Its Environment in Sri

Lanka." Abacus, 11 (June 1975), 86-96.
The author concludes that, for accounting to be able to
contribute its share in solving the problems of economic
development in Sri Lanka, prospective accountants will have
to be provided with a broad educational background through
universities and technical colleges.

Sherk, Donald R. "The Case For Foreign Investment in Asia:
Japan vs. the U.S." Columbia Journal of World Business, 9
(Fall 1974), 95-104.
The nations of developing Asia comprise a region in which
the companies of Japan and the United States increasingly
confront each other. The author discusses this confrontation and its meaning for the developing host countries
of Asia.

Singh, D.R. "Capital Budgeting and Indian Investment in
Foreign Countries." Management International Review, 17
(1977/1), 101-110.
This study examines the capital budgeting practices of Indian companies with joint ventures abroad. The study identifies and evaluates the objective of starting manufacturing operations by Indian companies in foreign countries,
authority for making policy decisions for their foreign
subsidiaries, techniques used for the evaluation of international investment decisions, various environmental risks,
and techniques for minimizing these risks, based on a
questionnaire survey.

Travers, Nicolas. "Financial Reporting in the Japanese
Company." Accountancy, 86 (January 1975), 34-36.
The author reports that understanding the Japanese accounting system requires a working knowledge of modern Japanese
history and commercial practice. He points out several
areas in which Japanese accounting practices differ from
American.

Treadwell, B.J. "Japan's New Foreign Exchange and Foreign
Trade Control Law--Does it Help the Foreign Investor?"
The Australian Accountant, 51 (November 1981), 676-680.
This article outlines and discusses the amendment to the
Japan's Foreign Exchange and Foreign Trade Control Law of
1949, reviews the operation of the amended law to date,
and considers whether the amended rules and procedures
assist the foreign investor interested in making direct
domestic investment in Japan.

Yamakawa, Thomas T. "How the Strong Yen Influenced Financial Reporting in Japan." Management Accounting, 60

(June 1979), 26-31.
The author points out that because of exchange controls in
Japan, hedging opportunities are limited and simply struc-
tured. These and other factors, such as some flexibility
allowed in the tax rule, make the Japanese tax aspects of
foreign exchange transactions generally less onerous than
those in the United States.

Yung, Sanford Y.T. "The Hong Kong Securities Commission."
The Accountant's Magazine, 82 (April 1978), 153-155.
In the space of five years the Hong Kong Government has established a solid foundation on which the securities industry there can effectively function. Companies must disclose
more in their annual accounts than ever before and have to
consolidate if they have subsidiaries. This article explains some recent achievements in a continuing program of
change.

Australia and New Zealand

Chambers, R.J. "A Critical Examination of Australian Accounting Standards." Abacus, 11 (December 1975), 136-152.
This paper was presented at the 1975 Annual Congress of the
Western Australian Branch of the Institute of Chartered Accountants in Australia. The author discusses the development ana applicability of professional standards.

Fisher, John E. "Establishment of Foreign Operations in
Australia." The Chartered Accountant in Australia, 49
(October 1978), 11-23.
The purpose of this report is to outline political, economic, social and legislative factors for consideration by
non-residents who may be contemplating investment or business activity in Australia.

Francis, J.R., and B.M. Pollard. "An Investigation of Nonaudit Fees in Australia." Abacus, 15 (December 1979), 136-
144.
This study describes the relative level of nonaudit fees
paid by Australian public companies to their auditors.
Some studies of nonaudit services are reviewed in order to
assess what is currently known about the compatibility of
nonaudit services and the independent attest function.

Gilling, D.M., and P.J. Stanton. "Changes in the Structure
of the Auditing Profession in Australia." Abacus, 14 (June
1978), 66-80.
The authors present the results of a study of the structure

of the auditing profession in Australia, and the changes
that have occurred in that structure during the years 1971
to 1976. The data presented show a pattern of increasing
concentration, dominance by a few firms and increasing size
inequality between largest and smallest firms.

Gniewosz, G. "The Equity Method of Accounting for Investments in Common Stock: The New Zealand Experience." The
International Journal of Accounting Education and Research,
15 (Spring 1980), 115-128.
The objectives of this article are to state the position
in New Zealand regarding the equity method of accounting
for investments in common stock and to highlight some of
the main differences with APB No. 18 and the pronouncements
and exposure drafts in certain other English-speaking countries, and to report the financial reporting practice of
New Zealand-listed public corporations in the light of the
recommendations of SSAP No. 2.

Graham, A.W. "Australia: Experiment in Cooperation." The
Accountant's Magazine, 78 (January 1974), 25-27.
This article describes the accountancy profession in Australia, and focuses on the high measure of cooperation between The Institute of Chartered Accountants in Australia
and the Australian Society of Accountants.

Harrison, B.G. "Accountancy in New Zealand." Accountancy,
84 (December 1973), 14-17.
This article is the first of a two-part series on the unique
conditions in which the profession has developed in Australia and New Zealand. Accountancy education in New Zealand
is described here.

Harrison, B.G. "Australia and the Value of Cooperation."
Accountancy, 85 (January 1974), 38-40.
This is the second of a two-part article on accounting in
Australia and New Zealand. The author discusses profes-
sional education and training in Australia.

Juchau, Roger. "Accounting Practice Problems in Papua New
Guinea and Fiji." The Australian Accountant, 48 (March
1978), 110-113.
The author reports the results of a questionnaire survey
among qualified accountants with current work experience in
Papua, New Guinea and Fiji. This survey was directed at
finding out what the accountants felt were the most serious
problems in practicing in Papua, New Guinea and Fiji.

McCrann, T. "Developments in Australian Company Reporting."

The Australian Accountant, 51 (September 1981), 531-533.
The author discusses developments in Australian corporate
reporting, and makes some practical suggestions for the
future.

Page, Neville B. "An Australian Dollar Exchange Market."
The Australian Accountant, 48 (July 1978), 367-372.
The author discusses his reasons for believing it would be
in the national interest to establish an Australian dollar
exchange market on the basis of a small number of licensed
currency dealers under the control of the Reserve Bank.

Parker, R.H. "Reforming Company Financial Reporting: Some
Recent Australian Views." The Accountant's Magazine, 79
(October 1975), 347-348.
In this article, the author briefly reviews some recent
Australian publications covering the possible establish-
ment of a Corporation and Securities Commission, the pres-
cription of rules of asset valuation by statute, accounting
for inflation, and profit forecast.

Trow, Donald G., and Stephen A. Zeff. "Recent Developments
in Financial Reporting in New Zealand." The Accountant's
Magazine, 80 (September 1976), 342-344.
Consideration of various approaches to inflation accounting
and implementation of a controversial Statement of Standard
Accounting Practice on Depreciation have been the main features of many interesting developments in financial reporting activity in New Zealand.

Wasley, Robert S. "The Role of Management Accounting in
New Zealand Business." The International Journal of Accounting Education and Research, 10 (Spring 1975), 57-74.
Some years ago, the author surveyed by personal interview
twenty-two New Zealand business firms to ascertain the extent to which management accounting concepts and ideas were
being applied. The author has repeated this process to determine what changes have occurred.

Whittred, G.P. "Australian Accounting Standards--Some
Anomalies." The Australian Accountant, 48 (September 1978),
498-503.
The author discusses the differences between International
Accounting Standard 9, Accounting for Research and Develop-
ment Activities, and (Australian) Statement of Accounting
Standards DS 12/308, Accounting for the Extractive Indus-
tries.

Canada

Boersema, John. "Corporate Reporting in Canada and the
US." CA Magazine, 114 (July 1981), 30-35.
The author concludes that the US standard-setting process
suggests that its results to date are not necessarily inap-
propriate for Canada and, in fact, can offer significant
and useful input into further Canadian developments.

Drury, D.H. "Effects of Accounting Practice Divergence:
Canada and the USA." Journal of International Business
Studies, 10 (Fall 1979), 75-87.
This paper illustrates the differences between U.S. and
Canadian accounting practices and examines empirically the
effects of supplying divergent information to Canadian and
U.S. investors. The implications for U.S. investors in
Canada and the impact on the future of development of finan-
cial reporting for foreign investors are examined.

Holmes, Geoffrey. "Focus on a Canadian Giant." Accountancy, 85 (May 1974), 76-80.
The author examines the accounts of Massey-Ferguson, a Canadian company with factories worldwide. Even though Canadian, the company reports in American dollars.

Kohlhagen, Steven W. "The Stability of Exchange Rate Expectations and Canadian Capital Flows." The Journal of
Finance, 32 (December 1977), 1657-1669.
The author specifies exchange rate expectations as a function of real economic variables that are endogenous to a
fully specified Kouri-Porter type model of capital flows.

McMonnies, Peter. "Accounting Standards At a Crossroad."
The Accountant's Magazine, 85 (February 1981), 38-40.
The Canadian Institute of Chartered Accountants has contributed to the debate about accounting standards with a
recently published research study. Here, the author views
the study and adds some thoughts of his own on this important subject which affects accountants worldwide.

Turner, John N. "Canada and Economic Reality: Accountants
Have A Part To Play." The Accountant, 177 (22/29 December
1977), 797-798.
The author contends that Canada must move its manufacturing
into the post-industrial world, broaden the scope of its
services and professions, and revive the growth of its resource industries. He then discusses ways in which accountants can help to achieve these goals.

125

Baxter, W.T. "Case Studies in South American Business 1: Coping with High Inflation in Argentina." The Accountant, 175 (4 November 1976), 526-527.
This article deals with the problem of accounting in a highly-inflationary economy, using historical cost accounting.

Baxter, W.T. "Case Studies in South American Business 2: Revolution and Counter-Revolution in Chile." The Accountant, 175 (18 November 1976), 587-588.
This article deals with the advantages of inflation accounting in a highly inflationary economy.

Baxter, W.T. "Case Studies in South American Business 3: Exhilaration of Growth in Brazil." The Accountant, 175 (9 December 1976), 676-678.
The author presents the hypothetical case of a British company that has bought an interest in a Brazilian company. The chief features of the reformed accounting system in use in Brazil are described.

Baxter, W.T. "Case Studies in South American Business 4: Workers Taking Over in Peru." The Accountant, 175 (23/30 December 1976), 734-735.
This case illustrates the problems involved in doing business with Peru.

Chu, José Manuel. "Accounting Principles and Practices in Panama." The International Journal of Accounting Education and Research, 9 (Fall 1973), 43-52.
The author discusses Panamanian accounting practices. He also compares practices used by Panama with those used in the U.S. This article also contains a brief description of auditing practices in Panama and an example of Panamanian financial statements.

Errunza, Vihang R. "Determinants of Financial Structure in the Central American Common Market." Financial Management, 8 (Autumn 1979), 72-77.
This paper studies the financial structure of firms domiciled in the Central American Common Market. The results support the hypothesis that there are statistically significant differences in the financial structure of different industries in this region and that country norms are less important than industry norms.

Huber, Richard L. "Brazil's Formula for Economic Growth."

Columbia Journal of World Business, 7 (March/April 1972), 57–62.
The author describes Brazil's system for coping with inflation--rationalized distribution of the effects of inflation, fiscal incentive programs for the development of remote regions and backward industries, and a favorable attitude toward foreign investment.

McMahon, Terrence J. "Brazil: A Maturing Capital Market Seeks Accelerated Improvements in Accountancy." The International Journal of Accounting Education and Research, 8 (Fall 1972), 77–87.
The Central Bank of Brazil has taken the initial steps needed to permit the accounting profession to develop self-regulation. Accountants will play an active, essential role in the launching of FUMCAP, a $50 million revolving Capital Market Development Fund. The author discusses advantages of a successful FUMCAP.

Mepham, Michael J. "The Accountancy Profession in Jamaica." The Accountant's Magazine, 81 (November 1977), 468–470.
This article describes the origins and development of the accountancy profession in Jamaica and outlines how it is organized today.

Moir, Roger J. "Cayman Island: Tax Haven or Financial Centre?" The Accountant's Magazine, 79 (May 1975), 182–183.
From a taxation viewpoint, Cayman Island provides an instrument by which people can minimize excessive tax burdens by effective tax planning, within the bounds of the law as it applies to their country and Cayman Island.

Mora, Ricardo E., Jr. "The Accounting Profession in Mexico--And Why." The International Journal of Accounting Education and Research, 11 (Spring 1976), 143–177.
The author outlines the history and structure of the accountancy profession in Mexico. He also discusses Mexican audit reports and accounting principles.

Peña, Pablo A. "Special Report: A Comparison of the Accounting Professions of Colombia and the United States." The International Journal of Accounting Education and Research, 11 (Spring 1976), 143–177.
This paper continues the study of Colombian accounting development after 1956. Conclusions are presented summarizing the basis for the formulation of an educational program oriented to satisfy the most urgent requirements of the accounting profession in Colombia.

Radebaugh, Lee H. "Environmental Factors Influencing the Development of Accounting Objectives, Standards, and Practices in Peru." The International Journal of Accounting Education and Research, 11 (Fall 1975), 39-56.
The author analyzes accounting in Peru, presenting a description of the current state of the art, and also a discussion of the changes in accounting objectives, standards, and practices, what factors led to those changes, and how these changes were accomplished.

Whitt, John D. "Multinationals in Latin America: An Accent on Control." Management Accounting, 58 (February 1977), 49-54.
This article concerns a survey of the headquarters of MNCs with Latin American operations and of Latin American subsidiaries of United States MNCs. The survey analyzes the problems of financial control in Latin American operations.

Whitt, John D. "Motivating Lower-Level Management of Mexican Affiliates." Management Accounting, 60 (June 1979), 46-49.
The author reports the results of a survey to test the hypothesis that Mexican affiliates of United States multinational firms do not allow or require participation of lower level management in financial planning and control to the extent followed in the U.S. affiliates.

Zeff, Stephen A., and Manuel Torres. "Mexico: Recent Developments in Accounting Standards." The Accountant's Magazine, 78 (May 1974), 180-181.
This article describes the accounting profession in Mexico.

Developing Countries

Abdeen, Adnan. "The Role of Accounting in Project Evaluation and Control: The Syrian Experience." The International Journal of Accounting Education and Research, 15 (Spring 1980), 143-158.
This paper focuses on the role of accounting techniques and practices in the evolution of capital investment decisions. It introduces the reader to the evaluation and decision-making process used to select industrial projects as practices in the developing country of the Syrian Arab Republic.

Barkas, James M., and James C. Gale. "Joint Venture Strategies: Yugoslavia A Case Study." Columbia Journal of World Business, 16 (Spring 1981), 30-39.
This article examines the objectives a MNC should consider

in developing an investment strategy for one developing country with a high growth rate, Yugoslavia. It also discusses certain criteria useful in evaluating the risks to the proposed projects' cash flow.

Briston, Richard J. "The Accountancy Profession in a Developing Country: An Indonesian Case Study." The Accountant's Magazine, 78 (August 1974), 314-315.
This article is the result of a visit to Indonesia on behalf of the British Government to examine ways in which it might be possible to assist in the training of Indonesian accountants and financial managers. The author describes the accounting needs of Indonesia, and ways they are being satisfied.

Briston, Richard J. "The Evolution of Accounting in Developing Countries." The International Journal of Accounting Education and Research, 14 (Fall 1978), 105-120.
The author concludes that each country should be encouraged not to standardize the structure and specifications of its information system, but to create a system appropriate to its own needs.

Dorian, Daniel G. "Management Accounting in a Developing Country." Management Accounting, 55 (May 1974), 15-18, 24.
The author suggests that accountants can help both the people of developing countries by promoting better economic conditions and also their own companies by providing profitable new sources of production and marketing opportunities.

Elliott, Edward L. "Accounting and Economic Development in Latin America." The International Journal of Accounting Education and Research, 8 (Fall 1972), 89-97.
While the emphasis in this paper is on Latin America, the author states that many of the ideas presented can be applied to developing areas in general. The author believes that the accountant should participate at all levels in the process of economic development.

Enthoven, Adolf J.H. "Standardized Accountancy and Economic Development." Management Accounting, 57 (February 1976), 19-23.
The author discusses the scope and methods of standardization in social, government, and enterprise accounting, and within the overall accounting framework. Then he suggests how improved international accounting standards and conventions might be attained.

Enthoven, A.J.H. "The Scope for Accountancy Planning in

Developing Countries." Accounting and Business Research, 6 (Spring 1976), 135-139.
This article outlines an inventory of the requirements needed for a good accounting system for the less developed nations.

Enthoven, Adolf J.H. "The Accountant in the Third World." The Journal of Accountancy, 149 (March 1980), 76-78.
This is an adaptation of a speech on accounting in economic development management. The author elaborates on the role that the accounting profession and the accounting educator can play in developing countries.

Foroughi, Tahirih Khodadoust. "Accounting in Developing Countries Before and After Social Crisis: The Case of Iran." The International Journal of Accounting Education and Research, 17 (Fall 1981), 181-223.
This article examines the status of accounting education and of the profession in Iran before the 1978-79 crisis and after. An examination of the problems, changes, and challenges of Iranian accounting is presented.

Gabriel, Peter P. "MNCs in the Third World: Is Conflict Unavoidable?" Harvard Business Review, 50 (July/August 1972), 93-102.
Though the record may justify the conclusion that eventual confrontation between a MNC and the government of a less developed nation is inevitable, harmony remains in the interest of both. The author suggests a rationale for coexistence: relieving the company of the risk of asset investment and committing the host country by contract to honor the agreement.

Heenan, David A., and Warren J. Keegan. "The Rise of Third World Multinationals." Harvard Business Review, 57 (January-February 1979), 101-109.
The authors answer questions like where the third world MNCs come from, where they are going, and why they are so unlike their predecessors in the developed countries.

Holzer, H. Peter, and Doria Tremblay. "Accounting and Economic Development: The Cases of Thailand and Tunisia." The International Journal of Accounting Education and Research, 9 (Fall 1973), 67-80.
The purpose of this article is to outline the need for accounting in a developing country. It also includes an analysis of the status of accounting in Thailand and Tunisia for illustrating how the needs for accounting are or are not being met in two specific developing nations.

Holzer, H. Peter, and John S. Chandler. "A System Approach to Accounting in Developing Countries." Management International Review, 21 (1981/4), 23-32.
The authors state that the accounting establishment in developing countries consists of indigenous enterprises, the local accounting profession, government, and educational institutions. They then propose a system solution whereby underlying problems are identified and attacked.

Jaggi, B.L. "Accounting Studies of Developing Countries." The International Journal of Accounting Education and Research, 9 (Fall 1973), 159-170.
The authors assess what has been done and examines the potential for further research in accounting problems of developing countries. He concludes that an immediate need exists for descriptive studies of various countries in order to develop conceptual and hypothesis-testing studies.

Kafka, Alexandre. "The New Exchange Rate Regime and the Developing Countries." The Journal of Finance, 33 (June 1978), 795-802.
The author discusses three aspects of the experience of LDCs since the advent of the new exchange rate regime. These aspects are the short term variabilities of exchange rates, real exchange rates, and reserve use. The results confirm expectations based on conventional theory.

Lelievre, Clara C., and Thomas W. Lelievre. "Accounting in the Third World." The Woman CPA, 39 (October 1977), 3-5.
This article describes the problems faced by the accounting profession in the developing countries.

Lelievre, Thomas W., and Clara C. Lelievre. "Accounting in the Third World." The Journal of Accountancy, 145 (January 1978), 72-75.
This article examines the relationship between some of the problems of emerging nations, the underutilization of managerial accounting techniques, and the lack of adequate measurement and reporting standards. It focuses on African nations, but all developing countries share many common goals and problems.

Ogan, Pekin. "Turkish Accountancy: An Assessment of Its Effectiveness and Recommendations for Improvements." The International Journal of Accounting Education and Research, 14 (Fall 1978), 133-156.
This article describes the degree of effectiveness of gathering and reporting of accounting information in Turkey. Comparisons of Turkish accountancy with those of similarly

developing nations are made where appropriate to highlight
similarities or to draw attention to the unique Turkish
situation.

Qureshi, Mahmood A. "Private Enterprise Accounting and
Economic Development in Pakistan." The International Journal of Accounting Education and Research, 9 (Spring 1974),
125-142.
The main objective of this study is to investigate the potential of private enterprise accounting as a tool in the
development of an emerging economy, such as Pakistan. The
study encompasses capital formation, foreign investment,
and management capability.

Rogness, Earl C. "For Export: Accounting Expertise."
Management Accounting, 58 (January 1977), 19-20.
In developing countries one can most often find the wil-
lingness to work, but persons with education and skills
needed to give direction are in short supply. Writing from
his own experience, the author tells how he assisted in
bringing accounting know-how to two developing countries:
El Salvador and Iran.

Shuaib, Shuaib A. "Accounting Information and the Development Planning Process in Kuwait." The International Journal of Accounting Education and Research, 15 (Spring 1980),
129-141.
This study investigates the information requirements of the
development planning process in Kuwait and identifies areas
where improvements in accounting practices are needed to
facilitate the attainment of national economic goals.

Whiteley, John. "Third World Aid--How and Why Are We Going
Wrong?" Accountancy, 87 (August 1976), 42-44.
The author's main theme is that nothing will be achieved
in the direction of developing the underdeveloped countries
of the world and closing the gap between rich and poor nations until the great mass of people in the rich countries
can see the inequalities from the other person's point of
view.

Europe

Belgium

Asselman, Roger J. "Accounting in Belgium and Luxembourg."
Accountancy, 83 (April 1973), 10-16.
The author describes the manner in which the accountancy

132

profession is organized in these two EEC countries.

Bent, F.T., E. Cracco, and R. Vuerings. "The Belgian Environment for Multinational Business: Conflicting Perspectives." Columbia Journal of World Business, 10 (Fall 1975),
119-130.
In assessing the climate for foreign investment, managers
of MNCs must evaluate more than just economic trends. The
authors examine how managers of U.S. subsidiaries located
in Belgium collect and evaluate such information and the
different perspectives U.S. managers and their Belgium col-
leagues have of the foreign investment climate.

Lefebvre, Chris J.L. "Development of Belgian Accounting
Standards Within the European Economic Community Framework." The International Journal of Accounting Education
and Research, 17 (Fall 1981), 103-132.
This paper outlines some considerations on the accounting
situation within the European Economic Community and some
observations on the Belgian accounting environment.

Denmark

Olsen, B. Niemann. "The Accountancy Profession in Denmark."
The Accountant's Magazine, 81 (June 1977), 257-259.
The Director of the Danish Institute describes the structure of the accounting profession in his country, its approach to standard-setting and to its widening responsibilities, and the part its members play in the country's
taxation system.

Peterson, Arne From. "The Accounting Profession in Denmark." Accountancy, 85 (February 1974), 34-42.
The author discusses education and certification of accountants in Denmark, as well as services provided by accountants.

France

Altman, Edward I., Bertrand Jacquillat, and Michel Levasseur. "Comparative Analysis of Risk Measures: France and
the United States." The Journal of Finance, 29 (December
1974), 1495-1511.
The purpose of this paper is to examine, on a comprehensive basis, the market model for the French Stock Market
and to compare on an exact basis the results with equivalent U.S. studies.

Barbier, Guy. "Accounting in France." Accountancy, 83 (October 1972), 10-17.
The organization of the accounting profession in France is described.

Barrett, M.E., and J. Roy. "Financial Reporting in France." Financial Analysts Journal, 32 (January/February 1976), 39-49.
This article discusses various aspects of financial reporting and analysis in France. The approach to the subject is conceptual. From time to time, however, suggestions of a practical nature have been interjected where these may guide the American analyst.

Collins, Lionel. "The New Dynamics of French Accounting." The Accountant, 182 (5 June 1980), 829-831.
The author discusses various changes that have occurred in recent years in accounting and auditing in France. He predicts that, in France, public accounting and auditing will be very much a growth industry in the next decade.

Filos, V.P. "Some Noteworthy Theories from the French and Swiss Tradition in Accounting." Accounting and Business Research, 11 (Autumn 1981), 267-279.
This paper provides an introduction to the theories of some outstanding French accounting theorists. The Swiss accounting historian and theorist, Leon Gomberg, and his views are also included, since they are quite pertinent to the French tradition as well as opposing the business economics school.

Germany

Goettsche, Hans G. "Accounting in Germany." Accountancy, 83 (August 1972), 24-31.
The author describes the development, organization, standards and practices of the accountancy profession in Germany.

Hole, Roderick C., and Michael A. Alkier. "German Financial Statements." Management Accounting, 56 (July 1974), 28-34.
The German versions of two business reports, the balance sheet and the statement of profit and loss, are commented upon by the authors and comparisons are made with the U.S. counterparts of these reports. The formats which are specified by law are illustrated in the article.

Kern, Werner. "The Accounting Concept in German Labor-Oriented Business Management." The International Journal of Accounting Education and Research, 10 (Spring 1975), 23-35.
This paper deals with AOEWL (Arbeitsorientierte Einzel-wirtschaftslahre) demands for the accounting area.

Lück, Wolfgang. "Recent Changes in the German Professional Certified Public Accountant (Wirtschaftsprüfer) Examination." The International Journal of Accounting Education and Research, 13 (Fall 1977), 131-140.
This article outlines recent changes in the German professional certified public accountants examination.

Niehus, Rudolf J. "Germany Updates Its Standards." The Accountant, 176 (26 May 1977), 604-605.
The German Institut der Wirtschaftsprüfer (Institute of Public Accountants) promulgated its first statement of auditing standards in 1967, two years after the new stock corporation law (Aktiengesetz) went into effect.

Schoenfeld, Hanns-Martin. "Development and Present State of Cost Theory in Germany." The International Journal of Accounting Education and Research, 8 (Fall 1972), 43-65.
This article provides an analysis of cost determinants; it also shows that the model-building process to develop cost functions can be continued, eventually resulting in uni-quely defined modular components of cost function that can be applied directly in various environments. The European microeconomics-based approach suggests that certain steps toward closing the gap between operations research and de-cision models on the one hand and management accounting on the other have already been taken.

Smith, G.R. "German Federal Republic." The Accountant's Magazine, 79 (August 1975), 283-286.
The author outlines the development of the accounting pro-fession in Germany, and analyzes some recent developments in accounting thought. His analysis includes the role of forecasts, and inflation accounting. He also compares the development of accounting thought in Germany with that of the UK and the USA.

Greece

Costouros, George J. "Accounting Education and Practice in Greece." The International Journal of Accounting Education and Research, 11 (Fall 1975), 95-106.

The author provides some historical background and a discussion of current educational practices. He states that the teaching of accounting has contributed substantially in serving the continuously increasing socio-economic and professional needs of Greece.

Hadjinicolaou, Yiangos. "Greece: Package Deals For Multinationals." Accountancy, 90 (April 1979), 76-77.
The author advises that, if you are looking for a base in the Middle East, to try Greece for the best tax advantage.

Holland

Beekhuizen, Theo, and Paul Frishkoff. "A Comparison of the New Dutch Accounting Act With Generally Accepted American Accounting Principles." The International Journal of Accounting Education and Research, 10 (Spring 1975), 13-22.
The authors employ a descriptive approach in their comparative analysis of accounting principles in the Netherlands and the United States.

deMare, H.B. "New Rules of Conduct and Professional Activities in the Netherlands." The Accountant's Magazine, 78 (July 1974), 273-275.
This article provides a summary of 1973 revisions in the Rules of Conduct and Professional Activities of the Nederlands Institunt van Registeraccountants.

Klaassen, Jan. "An Accounting Court: The Impact of the Enterprise Chamber on Financial Reporting in the Netherlands." The Accounting Review, 55 (April 1980), 327-341.
A unique feature of the institutional framework of financial reporting in the Netherlands is the recent introduction of an Enterprise Chamber to settle disputes between companies and parties interested in their financial statements. This article describes the Chamber and evaluates its significance.

Knol, Alfred W. "Accounting in Holland." Accountancy, 83 (January 1973), 32-38.
The accounting profession in Holland is described.

Van Rossem, J.P. "Annual Accounts in The Netherlands." The Accountant, 174 (17 June 1976), 708-710.
The author discusses the experience of employers, trade unions and the accounting profession in the cooperative development of accounting standards in the Netherlands.

Volten, Henk. "Continuing Education in the Netherlands."
The Accountant's Magazine, 80 (December 1976), 474-475.
The author discusses the importance of Post-Qualification
Education, and what is being done in the Netherlands.

Italy

Christie, Hugh. "Italy--Planning for the 1980's." The
Accountant's Magazine, 82 (August 1978), 343-344.
This article reports on some recent developments on the
Italian accounting scene. The author concludes that the
change that is happening in the Italian profession on the
one hand, and in Italian business and industry on the
other, should ultimately strengthen both spheres of
activity.

Tenz, Walter. "Accounting in Italy." Accountancy, 83 (November 1972), 20-30.
The author describes the organization of the accounting
profession in Italy.

Zappala, Frederick J. "The Current State of the Accounting
Profession in Italy." The International Journal of Accounting Education and Research, 8 (Spring 1973), 111-121.
The author spent several months in Italy visiting major
international firms, and Italian firms and universities.
This paper, the result of many discussions with professional accountants, university professors, and students, represents a consensus of opinion on existing conditions.

Portugal

Blackshaw, Ian. "Foreign Investment in Portugal." The
Accountant, 182 (17 April 1980), 568-569.
The author discusses the Foreign Investment Code, compri-
sing Decree-Law No. 348/77 of August 24, 1977, and supplementary regulations issued in the form of Decrees at
the same time; foreign investment in Portugal is governed
basically by this law.

Spain

Blackshaw, Ian S. "Doing Business in Spain: Some Accounting Aspects." The Accountant, 181 (20 September 1979),
387-389.
This article, in summarizing the present state of the

accounting art in Spain, is confined to the accounting and
auditing requirements of joint stock companies which, for
various legal and practical reasons, are the most popular
vehicles for foreign direct investment in Spain.

McCrossin, Francis. "Spain: Country At the Crossroads."
The Accountant's Magazine, 79 (February 1975), 81-83.
The author describes the weather, history, and geography
as well as what it is like to live and work in Spain, particularly from an accounting point of view. His description includes the state of the economy, the accounting
profession and accounting principles in Spain.

United Kingdom

Aranya, Nissim. "The Influence of Pressure Groups on Financial Statements in Britain." Abacus, 10 (June 1974),
3-12.
This paper suggests that the development of financial statements is affected by the conflicting interests of its sup-
pliers (management), its consumers (mainly shareholders and
creditors), regulatory agencies and accounting bodies.
These changing interests are reflected in the changing in-
terpretation of the auditor's role.

Blake, Nicholas. "UK and US Standards--A Comparison."
Accountancy, 90 (September 1979), 50-55.
The author makes a comparison between the Standard-setting
bodies and the method of compiling and issuing an accounting Standard, both in the UK and also in the US.

Climo, Tom. "What's Happening in Britain?" The Journal
of Accountancy, 141 (February 1976), 55-59.
Determining the objectives of financial statements is a
necessary precondition to the successful application of accounting standards. The author discusses THE CORPORATE RE-
PORT and its significance to the accounting profession. He
sees The Report as an indicator that the accounting profession has taken a huge step forward.

Comiskey, Eugene E., and Roger E.V. Groves. "United Kingdom Developments in Interperiod Tax Allocation." The International Journal of Accounting Education and Research,
16 (Spring 1981), 1-11.
This article identifies the more typical UK timing differences and provides illustrations of how companies have dealt
with them in adapting to SSAP No. 15. Some thoughts are
offered on the relative merits of the current disparate

positions of the accounting profession in the United States and the United Kingdom on this issue.

Hodges, S.D., and R.A. Brealey. "The Rate of Return on New Investment in the UK." The Journal of Finance, 35 (June 1980), 799-800.
The author provides striking new evidence that the profitability of British industry is currently much lower than anyone had previously supposed.

Konrath, Larry F. "Auditing Practices in the Republic of Ireland: An Environmental Approach." Management International Review, 14 (1974/4-5), 105-110.
The purpose of this study is to test the extent to which differing environmental factors affect auditing standards and procedures. It tests the hypothesis that the auditing environment in the Republic of Ireland is different from the auditing environment in the United States and, therefore, auditing standards and procedures are different between the two countries.

Mitchell, Keith R. "The United Kingdom Profession: Hydebound and Crossed." The Australian Accountant, 48 (March 1978), 84-86.
The author explains the Hyde Guidelines on the implementation of current cost accounting.

Parker, R.H. "British Men of Account." Abacus, 14 (June 1978), 53-65.
The author discusses accountants and the profession as an important part of history. He expounds the importance of accountants to present economic and social systems. The conclusion is that, since what accountants do is a response to the changing needs of society, it is in society's interest as well as their own that accountants should be educated for their responsibilities and not just trained as technicians.

Wanless, P.T. "Financial Reporting in Scotland: An Opinion Poll." The Accountant's Magazine, 78 (June 1974), 216-217.
This article is the result of a survey of Chartered Accountants in Scotland. The objective of the study was to ascertain whether or not methods used in financial reports in Scotland were likely to make Scottish financial reports not comparable with other UK reports.

Winjum, James O. "Income Tax Administration in Great Britain." The International Journal of Accounting Education and Research, 8 (Fall 1972), 109-116.

This paper describes the general administration of income taxes in Great Britain and in particular focuses on the respective roles played by the local tax inspector and the independent chartered accountant in the assessment of income taxes. In short, there is no audited tax return in Great Britain at this time, but the audit is an integral part of the tax return.

European Economic Community

Aggarwal, Raj. "International Differences in Capital Structure Norms: An Empirical Study of Large European Companies." Management International Review, 21 (1981/1), 75-88.
This paper examines the international determinants of capital structure among large European companies. Based on the data for the largest 500 European industrials, the results in this paper show that while size by itself or in conjunction with other variables is not a significant determinant of capital structure, both country and industry classification seem to be significant determinants of capital structure.

Bailey, Richard. "The Professions and the EEC." The Accountant, 179 (24 August 1978), 234-235.
This article explores the questions of whether or not professions have a contribution to make to EEC policy-making, and whether professions are currently given sufficient influence in EEC decision-making.

Bartholomew, E.G. "Harmonisation of Financial Reporting in the EEC." Accountancy, 90 (October 1979), 48-53.
The author describes how the Fourth Directive is significantly changing the accounts of all EEC states.

Bedford, Norton M., and Jacques P. Gautier. "An International Analytical Comparison of the Structure and Content of Annual Reports in the European Economic Community, Switzerland the the United States." The International Journal of Accounting Education and Research, 9 (Spring 1974), 1-44.
The purpose of this paper is to describe and examine the different information provided by contemporary annual reports released in the U.S., the EEC, and Switzerland. Emphasis is placed on differences in the accounting thought, principles, and procedures underlying national report preparation as they existed in 1973.

Blausten, Richard. "Life Assurance in the EEC: Implications for Accountants." The Accountant, 177 (1 September 1977), 252-253.
Membership of the EEC has opened up new markets for the UK's financial services sector. Many among the UK accounting profession realize the the potential of these markets should not be ignored.

Burnett, R. Andrew. "The Harmonization of Accounting Principles in the Member Countries of the European Economic Community." The International Journal of Accounting Education and Research, 11 (Fall 1975), 23-30.
The aim of this paper is to give some feel for the way in which the EEC harmonization of accounting policies is progressing, and the basic underlying thinking behind the whole harmonization process.

Cairns, David. "European Company Accounts." The Accountant's Magazine, 83 (May 1979), 211-212.
The first-ever survey of the reports and accounts of major European companies was published recently by the Financial Times. In this article, one of the joint authors summarizes some of its main findings.

Chang, Lucia S., and Kenneth S. Most. "International Accounting Standards: The Case of European Oil Companies." The International Journal of Accounting Education and Research, 12 (Fall 1976), 27-44.
The purpose of this study is to identify differences in accounting policies and practices revealed by oil industry companies in different European countries, in respect to matters for which the IASC has issued standards or exposure drafts.

Choi, Frederick D.S. "Financial Disclosure in Relation to the European Capital Market." The International Journal of Accounting Education and Research, 9 (Fall 1973), 53-66.
The purpose of this paper is to explore the question of whether financial disclosure and capital markets are related or are, in fact, uncongenial views in the continent of Europe. It is demonstrated in this article that financial disclosure and broadly based capital markets do indeed interrelate. Observations drawn from an international setting provide the principal evidence of this paper.

Choi, Frederick D.S. "European Disclosure: The Competetive Disclosure Hypothesis." Journal of International Business Studies, 5 (Fall 1974), 15-24.
This paper describes the effects which recent financing

developments in Europe have had upon the financial disclosure policy of a representative sample of leading European MNCs. The evidence presented in this article suggests the existence of a direct relationship between improved financial disclosure and entry into the international capital markets.

Fantl, Irving L. "Europe's Need: A Workable Capital Market." Financial Executive, 44 (September 1976), 22-30.
The author says that there is a vast difference between
the Anglo-American approach to corporate capitalization
and those practices found in continental Europe. The author outlines some of these differences and portrays the
changes taking place presently and to take place in the
near future.

Gibson-Moore, David. "UK Investor and Europe." Accountancy, 83 (January 1973), 79-84.
The author discusses some of the problems facing the European investor or analyst.

Gray, S.J. "European Investment Analysis." Accountancy,
88 (October 1977), 92-101.
This article examines the problem of disclosure facing the
international investor in European stock markets of varying
efficiency and developments.

Goddard, C.S., J.M. Samuels, and R.E.V. Groves. "Getting
Together in Europe." Accountancy, 84 (September 1973),
37-39.
This article reports on the findings of a research project
into European company finance. British businessmen might
find this useful when forming their plans for expansion
within the EEC.

Hewson, John, and Eisuke Sakakibara. "A Qualitative Analysis of Euro-Currency Controls." The Journal of Finance,
30 (May 1975), 377-400.
The purpose of this paper is to discuss the qualitative
effects of the imposition of various controls on the basis
of a general equilibrium portfolio model of the Euro-
dollar market. The analysis concentrates on the imposition
of reserve requirements on bank and nonbank foreign (Euro-
dollar) borrowing.

Hill, Christopher. "Innocent Among EEC Directives." Accountancy, 87 (August 1976), 96.
The author mentions some draft EEC financial Directives of
which accountants should be aware.

Jay, Douglas. "Counting the Cost of Our EEC Membership."
Accountancy, 87 (April 1976), 34-37.
The author points out that membership of EEC has a cost.
Some of these costs are then listed and discussed.

Lafferty, Michael. "Fourth Directive...What's In It For
Us?" Accountancy, 85 (July 1974), 30-32.
This is an interview of John Grenside, deputy president of
the English Institute, about the EEC harmonization procedures and the revised Fourth Directive.

Mahotiere, Stuart de la. "Britain and the EEC Now--A Provisional Balance Sheet." Accountancy, 87 (November 1976),
30-32.
The author looks at the very bad start which Britain has
made in economic terms as a member of the EEC.

McFarlane, Gravin. "The EEC Sixth Directive on Value Added
Tax: Alterations to the Law of the United Kingdom." The
Accountant's Magazine, 82 (January 1978), 18-20.
The author points out that the restatement of value added
tax now taking effect is of vital importance to the com-
mercial world and its advisors.

McLean, Alasdair T. "The EEC's Proposed Fourth Directive:
A Progress Report." The Accountant's Magazine, 80 (April
1976), 125-128.
Differences between British corporate reporting on the one
hand and continental European on the other are causing some
headaches for UK representatives in EEC working party ne-
gotiations over the European Commission's proposal for a
Fourth Directive concerning the accounting requirements
for companies in the EEC. This article explains the reasons
for the dialogue between the UK and Europe, and comments on
the implications of a Fourth Directive for the British accountancy profession.

McLean, Alasdair T. "Group Accounts in the EEC: A Look at
Some of the Proposals of the Draft Seventh Directive." The
Accountant's Magazine, 80 (June 1976), 211-212.
This article is about the proposed Seventh Directive of the
EEC, concerning group accounts. The author identifies some
of the main proposals of interest to accountants.

McMonnies, Peter N. "EEC Second Directive on Company Law."
The Accountant's Magazine, 81 (February 1977), 54-56.
The EEC Council of Ministers adopted the Second Directive
on company law on December 13, 1976. The purpose of this
article is to highlight what is likely to be new to the UK

as a result of the Second Directive, and, in addition, to outline briefly the area of company law which it covers.

Niehus, Rudolph. "Harmonized European Economic Community Accounting--A German View of the Draft Directive For Uniform Accounting Rules." The International Journal of Accounting Education and Research, 7 (Spring 1972), 91-115.
The author summarizes and evaluates the various provisions of the draft of the fourth directive of the EEC.

Nobes, C.W. "Harmonization of Accounting Within the European Communities: The Fourth Directive on Company Law." The International Journal of Accounting Education and Research, 15 (Spring 1980), 1-16.
This article summarizes the main causes of present national differences in accounting, discusses the purposes of harmonization, examines the EEC proposals for harmonization, and outlines the British government's response, particularly to the EEC's Fourth Directive on Company Law of July 1978.

O'Donovan, Vincent. "The European Dimension of Banking Market." The Accountant, 174 (25 March 1976), 351-353.
The author describes the efforts toward creating a genuine Common Market in financial services by the Brussels Commission and the Council of Ministers, the EEC's decision-making bodies.

O'Donovan, Vincent. "Coordination of Social Security Benefits Within the EEC." The Accountant, 174 (29 April 1976), 502-504.
Within the EEC, the term "coordination" is understood in a somewhat technical sense to apply to the bringing into proper relation of national social security systems for the benefit of nationals of one member state working in another. The wider issue of bringing about a closer comparability or compatibility between national systems is usually known under the term "harmonization." This article deals with the two terms as separate issues, proceeding from harmonization to coordination.

Parker, R.H. "A Slow Start to Company Harmonisation." Accountancy, 83 (June 1972), 26-29.
The author assesses the effects of the Common Market statutes on British company law.

Parker, R.H. "Group Accounts: Amending the Seventh Directive." The Accountant's Magazine, 83 (March 1979), 110-111.
The author provides a brief progress report on the EEC

Seventh Directive, which deals with group accounts.

Parker, R.H. "Questions and Answers on the Fourth Directive." The Accountant's Magazine, 82 (September 1978), 386-390.
The author provides, in question and answer form, a comprehensive guide to the important and fundamental changes the Directive will bring to British company accounts.

Periton. Paul. "The European Monetary System and its Relationship to the UK." The Accountant, 183 (28 August 1980), 348-351.
This article is a discussion of the European Monetary System, and the European Currency Unit as a denominator for expressing debts and claims between central banks.

Radford, Richard. "Harmonisation of Company Law: How it Works and Where it Stands." Accountancy, 91 (March 1980), 72-77.
The EEC is laying down minimum requirements which will form the basis of member states' national legislation. In the UK, the effect of EEC Directives on company law will be to switch control from a combination of legislation and self-regulation to control by statute. In this article, the author reviews the EEC's harmonization program and the current status of Directives. A flowchart is presented which shows how the Directive system works and at what stage each Directive has reached.

Radford, Richard. "Harmonisation of Company Law: Preparing for the Extra Burden." Accountancy, 91 (April 1980), 55-56.
This article outlines the main proposals of the draft Seventh and Eighth Directives, which deal with consolidations and professional qualifications. The author concludes that complex international group structures should be examined with an eye toward implementation of the Directives.

Seary, Bill. "EEC Finance--Is There Anything For Charities?" Accountancy, 92 (September 1981), 61-62.
The author shows how the European Social Fund works, and discusses some other ways of getting EEC funding.

Shirley, Robert. "The Common Market Prospectus." The Accountant's Magazine, 78 (November 1974), 437-440.
This article is based on a talk given by the author to the Wednesday Forum, at a meeting in Edinburgh on October 17, 1973. The author reviews main differences between the EEC

prospectus and the UK prospectus.

Stamp, Edward. "The EEC and European Accounting Standards: A Straitjacket or a Spur?" Accountancy, 83 (May 1973), 9-16.
The author believes that the influence of the EEC Commission will benefit the profession. He pays particular attention to harmonization of laws regulating the activities of companies, including the work of their auditors and accountants.

Tarrant, Nick. "Changes in Accounts for the EEC." Accountancy, 89 (October 1978), 145-147.
The author describes the accounting system introduced by the EEC Fourth Directive. The author refers to the fact that the Directive is designed to harmonize company law and accounts presentation through the EEC, but it will not in fact bring about complete uniformity.

Middle East

Abdel-Magid, Moustafa F. "The Theory of Islamic Banking: Accounting Implications." The International Journal of Accounting Education and Research, 17 (Fall 1981), 79-102.
The purpose of this paper is to provide a descriptive account of Islamic banking and explore its accounting implications. A brief introduction of the precepts and general principles of Islamic economics is included to place Islamic banking in its proper perspective.

AlHashim, Dhia D. "Social Accounting in Egypt." The International Journal of Accounting Education and Research, 12 (Spring 1977), 127-142.
The purposes of this paper are to highlight the main features of the uniform system of accounts as applied in one nation, Egypt, and to examine the effectiveness of this system in facilitating national planning and control.

Bait-El-Mal, Mohamed M., Charles H. Smith, and Martin E. Taylor. "The Development of Accounting in Libya." The International Journal of Accounting Education and Research, 8 (Spring 1973), 83-101.
The purpose of this paper is to describe the development of accounting, focusing on financial accounting, in the Libyan Arab Republic. Documentation of these developments can contribute to the literature of underdeveloped countries and to that of Africa in general.

El-Adly, Yousef A., and Mohamed A. El-Azma. "The Effects of Inflation on Kuwaiti Corporate Financial Statements." Journal of Contemporary Business, 9 (Third Quarter 1980), 109-122.
The purpose of this paper is twofold. First, the general features of inflation in the Kuwaiti economy is presented in order to appreciate the importance, from the accounting standpoint, of including this important variable. Second, a case study applying the general price level adjusted historical cost approach to the financial statements of a Kuwaiti company in the field of petrochemicals is undertaken.

Falk, Haim, Samuel Frumer, and James A. Heintz. "Accounting For Stock Reacquisitions: Israel and the United States Compared." The International Journal of Accounting Education and Research, 9 (Spring 1974), 111-124.
The purpose of this paper is to examine the treatment of transactions by a corporation of its own stock in the United States and in Israel. The legal points of view and accepted accounting procedures in both Israel and America are described and examined, and some deficiencies in each system are identified. A suggestion to improve the accepted procedures for accounting for stock reacquisitions is presented.

Lev, Baruch, and Baruch Yahalomi. "The Effect of Corporate Financial Statements on the Israeli Stock Exchange." Management International Review, 12 (1972/2-3), 145-150.
The authors use a technique that makes it possible to determine whether financial statements convey information to investors by comparing the volume of transaction at the vicinity of the date of release to the volume in the rest of the year. They conclude that the relevancy of financial statements to investors can be increased by shortening the time lag between the end of the reported period and the release of financial statements.

Lev, Baruch. "The Formulation of Accounting Standards and Rules: A Comparison of Efforts in Israel and the United States." The International Journal of Accounting Education and Research, 11 (Spring 1976), 121-131.
This article summarizes the Israeli experience in developing accounting standards and rules, compares this experience with that of the United States, and provides some general observations on the problem of accounting principles formulation.

Pointon, Leo. "Steering A Way Through the Saudi Maze."

Accountancy, 92 (June 1981), 127-128.
This article offers some advice to accountants working in
Saudi Arabia on how to minimize the difficulties which they
often face in meeting government requirements.

Shuaib, S.A., and David Went. "The Middle East: Accounting in Kuwait and a Banker's View of Business Opportunities in the Area." The Journal of Accountancy, 147 (November 1978), 74-79.
The first part of this article is based on a paper entitled,
"Accounting in Kuwait: Past, Present and Future," presented by Shuaib at the 1977 Annual Meeting of the American
Accounting Association. The author reports the current
status of the profession, and he recommends steps that
should be taken to improve the level of accounting in Kuwait. In the second part, Went focuses on the business opportunities that are now available for contractors in Saudi
Arabia and elsewhere in the Middle East. This second part
of the article is an adaptation of an article entitled,
"Doing Business in the Middle East--A Banker's View," originally published in Accountancy Ireland by David Went.

Shuaib, Shuaib A. "Accounting Information and the Development Planning Process in Kuwait." The International Journal of Accounting Education and Research, 15 (Spring 1980),
129-141.
This study investigates the information requirements of
the development planning process in Kuwait and identifies
areas where improvements in accounting practices are needed
to facilitate the attainment of national economic goals.

Shuaib, Shuaib A. "Some Aspects of Accounting Regulations
in Kuwait." Journal of Contemporary Business, 9 (Third
Quarter 1980), 85-99.
The purpose of this article is to analyze and evaluate reporting disclosure regulations in Kuwait and note areas
for improvement. The author first provides a general
analysis of accounting regulations in Kuwait, then surveys
some of the specific laws that relate to accounting practices; the survey provides background on the development
of accounting regulations in Kuwait.

Spinks, Nigel. "Foreign Investment: Move to the Middle
East Now." Accountancy, 87 (March 1976), 74-79.
This article is the first in a series by the author on
transacting business with the Middle East countries. Its
purpose is to discuss some of the legal and accounting
issues arising when firms start conducting business in the
Middle East.

Spinks, Nigel. "Foreign Business in Iran." Accountancy, 87 (April 1976), 66-69.
In this second in a series on transacting business with Middle East countries, the author analyzes the pros and cons of investing in Iran.

Spinks, Nigel. "Doing Business in the UAE." Accountancy, 87 (May 1976), 62-66.
The author examines one of the fastest developing societies in the world, and gives advice to potential investors.

Spinks, Nigel. "Foreign Investment: Doing Business in Saudi Arabia." Accountancy, 87 (June 1976), 88-91.
In the fourth and final article in this series on transacting business with Middle East countries, the author examines the pros and cons of dealing with oil-rich Saudi Arabia.

Wedley, William C. "Libya--Super-Rich, Labor-Poor." Columbia Journal of World Business, 9 (Summer 1974), 64-73.
The rapid changes brought to the Libyan economy from the discovery and exportation of petroleum have forced new problems on the country. The shortage of labor creates problems in attracting workers for planned development projects, thereby constraining growth in general. The author offers suggestions for institutional changes to ease these burdens.

Non-Market Countries

Bailey, D.T. "Enterprise Accounting in the USSR." Accounting and Business Research, 4 (Winter 1973), 43-59.
This article describes the history of accounting and bookkeeping in the USSR. It also explains the system used in the USSR for bookkeeping and cost accounting.

Bailey, D.T. "The Soviet Scene." The Accountant, 175 (5 August 1976), 154-156.
The author visited the USSR under the auspicies of the Anglo-Soviet Cultural Agreement, and this article is a result of that visit. This was done with an aim toward developing an understanding of the role of accounting in diverse economic and social environments.

Bailey, D.T. "The Accounting Profession in Russia." Accountancy, 88 (March 1977), 70-73.
The author surveys the recent history of the accountancy profession in the Soviet Union, and expresses the hope that

the time may not be far distant when Soviet specialists rejoin the international accounting community.

Bailey, D.T. "Marx on Accounting." The Accountant, 178 (5 January 1978), 12-14.
In The Accountant of 17 August 1963, Professor K.S. Most drew attention to the connection between Karl Marx and management accounting. The author feels it is time to attempt a reexamination and reevaluation of the extent and nature of that connection.

Bradley, Gene E. "East-West Trade." Columbia Journal of World Business, 8 (Winter 1973), 39-41.
Doing business with Socialist countries is dramatically different than in other markets and a series of seminars on this subject have been organized by the International Management and Development Institute. This article reviews the topics covered during the first seminar in New York and predicts that commercial ties may work not only for the benefit of the firm but also for the national interest.

Gorelik, George. "Notes on the Development and Problems of Soviet Uniform Accounting." The International Journal of Accounting Education and Research, 9 (Fall 1973), 135-148.
The purpose of this paper is to outline the historical development of Soviet uniform accounting and to consider some of the major problems that Soviet accounting is currently facing.

Gorelik, George. "Soviet Accounting, Planning and Control." Abacus, 10 (June 1974), 13-25.
The purpose of this paper is to describe the Soviet industrial planning and control system, to consider the role of accounting in this system, and to evaluate the effectiveness of Soviet accounting in planning and control decisions.

Hoyt, Ronald E. "Profit Measurement in East-West Trade and Industrial Cooperation: Concepts, Criteria, and Special Problems." The International Journal of Accounting Education and Research, 13 (Spring 1978), 119-144.
This article summarizes three models of product exchange as a basis for analyzing sources of profit in East-West trade transactions: Analytic Model of a Barter Transaction; Analytic Model of a Counterpurchase Transaction; and Analytic Model of a Compensation Agreement.

Hoyt, Ronald E., and Lawrence D. Maples. "Accounting For Joint Ventures With the Soviet Bloc and China." The International Journal of Accounting Education and Research,

16 (Fall 1980), 105–124.
The purpose of this paper is two-fold: first to examine
the implications of accounting for "joint ventures" between U.S. firms and public-sector enterprises in the Soviet Bloc and China; secondly, to provide an analysis of
tax implications for these types of ventures.

Jaruga, Alicja A. "Problems of Uniform Accounting Principles in Poland." The International Journal of Accounting Education and Research, 8 (Fall 1972), 25–41.
Uniform accounting principles have been developed in Poland
to meet the demands of planning and managing a national
economy. This article presents a description of the Polish
experiences and some aspects of the Uniform Accounting Plan
System.

Jaruga, Alicja A. "Recent Developments in Polish Accounting: An International Transaction Emphasis." The International Journal of Accounting Education and Research, 10
(Fall 1974), 1–18.
The author concentrates on the problems accompanying the
spectacular increase in Poland's foreign trade in recent
years related to the rapid development of Poland's economy,
and the topic of recent developments of Polish accounting.

Jaruga, Alicja A. "Recent Developments of the Auditing
Profession in Poland." The International Journal of Accounting Education and Research, 12 (Fall 1976), 101–110.
The author analyzes the development of the auditing profession in Poland with special emphasis on the peculiar and
typical features in social countries and the role the Polish Accountant's Association has played in the general
development.

Jaruga, Alicja A. "The Accountancy Profession in a Centrally Planned Economy: The Polish Case." The Accountant's
Magazine, 83 (October 1979), 428–430.
Professor Jaruga describes the structure of the accounting
profession in her country, its functions, duties and responsibilities and outlines the role played by chief accountants and state-authorized experts in accounting in a
centrally planned economy.

Kupzhasar, Naribaev. "Computer Applications in Soviet
Accounting." The International Journal of Accounting Education and Research, 10 (Fall 1974), 33–43.
The purpose of this paper is to discuss Soviet computer use
in accounting and its influence on organizational and
educational processes. In the Soviet Union, as in other

countries, accounting was the first of the management
functions to use computers.

Loeb, Martin, and Wesley A. Magat. "Soviet Success Indicators and the Evaluation of Divisional Management."
Journal of Accounting Research, 16 (Spring 1978), 103-121.
The purpose of this paper is to integrate the research of
Soviet success indicators with the study of such indicators
in the accounting literature, and to suggest a new indicator
for use in properly motivating enterprise or divisional
managers.

Maunders, K.T. "Financial Management in the Soviet Industrial Enterprise." Accounting and Business Research, 2
(Autumn 1972), 298-307.
The author gives a brief review of the present institutional
setup in Russia, a resume and comment on some of the important changes brought by the post-1965 reforms insofar as
they affect financial management, and concludes with an
examination of the possible effects of Soviet accounting
practices on some areas of financial decision making.

Motekat, Ula K. "The Accounting Cycle for a People-Owned
Enterprise." The Woman CPA, 41 (April 1979), 16-23.
This article is devoted to a description of the accounting
cycle for an East German manufacturing establishment.

Motekat, Ula K. "Prices In A Planned Economy." The Woman
CPA, 43 (October 1981), 30-33.
This article describes the Russian system of price deter-
mination by summarizing a recent book by Professor Dr. Juri
W. Jakowez. The Russian title of the book is Zeny W planowm
Chasjaistive; a German translation under the title, Die
Preise in der Planwirtschaft, published in East Germany
(Verlg Die Wirtschaft, Berlin, 1976) is the basis for this
article. This article is continued in the January 1982
issue.

Paraszczak, John. "Accounting Soviet Style." Management
Accounting, 60 (July 1978), 51-56.
The author describes and contrasts the accounting system in
the USSR with that of the USA. The author states that control is the primary function of accounting in the Soviet
Union. This is carried out by a system of highly regulated
and uniform accounting practices in both reporting and the
preparation of statements.

Satubaldin, Sagandyk. "Methods of Analyzing Profits of
Industrial Enterprises in the USSR." The International

Journal of Accounting Education and Research, 12 (Fall 1976), 91-100.
The author, head of the Department of Economic Analysis of the Alma-Ata Institute of National Economy in the Union of Soviet Socialist Republics, describes the methods used in analyzing profit of industrial enterprises in Russia.

Sawicki, Stanislaw J. "Evolution of Management Structures East and West: An Accountant's Overview." Journal of the Accounting Association of Australia and New Zealand, 18 (May 1978), 34-58.
The purposes of this paper are to describe some aspects of the system of accounting information which obtain in some countries that are conventionally described as being a centrally planned economy, and to examine the emphasis placed upon such aspects for management control systems in those countries.

Turk, Ivan. "Recent Professional Statements of Accounting Principles and Ethics in Yugoslavia." The International Journal of Accounting Education and Research, 12 (Fall 1976), 111-120.
This article describes the development of the accounting profession in Yugoslavia. It also outlines a summary of the Code of Ethical Conduct and of the Code of Accounting Principles in Yugoslavia.

Wortzel, Lawrence H. "Breaking Dependence on MNCs." Columbia Journal of World Business, 12 (Winter 1977), 86-95.
The author suggests strategies that locally-owned firms in the developing countries can adopt in building export businesses in manufactures. Recognition is given to the roles played by foreign investors and foreign subcontractors. Alternatives all involve local control and build on local strengths while compensating for major weaknesses.

Yang, Chi-Liang. "'Mass Line' Accounting in China." Management Accounting, 62 (May 1981), 13-21.
The author points out that the problem facing China's industrial managers was to devise an accounting system that would be understandable to the rank-and-file workers and that would motivate them to increase their productivity. Their solution: a unique responsibility accounting system based on principles drawn from the country's revolutionary past.

Ameiss, Albert P. "International Accounting at the Senior Student Level." The International Journal of Accounting Education and Research, 10 (Fall 1974), 107-121.
The author reports on the experiences the University of Missouri-St. Louis encountered in introducing and revising an undergraduate course in international accounting.

Brummet, R. Lee. "Internationalism and the Future of Accounting Education." The International Journal of Accounting Education and Research, 11 (Fall 1975), 161-165.
The author discusses educational needs of accounting students from an international perspective.

Burns, Jane O. "A Study of International Accounting Education in the United States." The International Journal of Accounting Education and Research, 15 (Fall 1979), 135-145.
To facilitate exchanges of ideas and course syllabi in international accounting, the Education Committee of the International Accounting Section of the AAA annually gathers syllabi from its members for distribution through the AAA Syllabus Exchange and for publication. This study is in response to needs expressed by faculty members teaching international accounting and by those whose schools desire to offer such a course.

Clay, Alvin A. "Undergraduate International Accounting Education." The International Journal of Accounting Education and Research, 11 (Fall 1975), 187-192.
The author discusses the undergraduate course in international accounting being taught at Villanova University.

Dascher, Paul E., Charles H. Smith, and Robert H. Strawser. "Accounting Curriculum Implications of the Multinational Corporation." The International Journal of Accounting Education and Research, 9 (Fall 1973), 81-98.
The objective of this paper is to identify some of the implications of the MNC as an influencing force for the future accounting curriculum. The study assumes that educators should develop a market orientation with respect to the performance of their function.

Dev, Susan, and Eno L. Inanga. "Educating Accountants in Nigeria." Accountancy, 90 (April 1979), 127-129.
The problem of meeting the demand for accountants in developing countries, and of deciding what forms of education and training are most appropriate to their needs, have attracted some attention in recent years. The purpose of

this article is to examine certain aspects in Nigeria.

Dewhurst, R.F.J. "Accountancy Education in South Africa."
The Accountant, 177 (15 December 1977), 759-760.
Accountancy education in South Africa differs from its
equivalent in the United Kingdom in one fundamental respect:
all paths to the qualification of "Chartered Accountant(SA)"
are through a university degree in accounting. The consequences in practice are substantial.

Dodden, Michael J. "First Thoughts on Secondment: An Innocent in Switaerland." Accountancy, 87 (April 1976), 56-
59.
The author describes the system that allows trainee chartered accountants to spend a six-month period of secondment in an overseas company.

Foutz, Paul B. "The Teaching of International Accounting."
Management Accounting, 56 (June 1975), 31-33.
The author states the need for the teaching of courses in
international accounting. Then he discusses some of the
problems involved in establishing and teaching the appropriate courses.

Kubin, Konrad W. "The Changing Nature of International
Accounting Courses." The International Journal of Accounting Education and Research, 9 (Fall 1973), 99-112.
This article outlines the historical development of the
international accounting course, and the recent changes
that have occurred to the course: its objectives; teaching
approach and method; and some implications for the future.

Lafferty, Michael. "Accountancy Education in Europe."
Accountancy, 86 (December 1975), 34-36.
The author compares education standards for becoming an
accountant in France, Germany, the Netherlands, Belgium,
Luxembourg, Denmark, Italy, the United Kingdom, and
Ireland.

Mintz, Steven M. "Internationalization of Accounting
Curriculum." The International Journal of Accounting Education and Research, 16 (Fall 1980), 138-151.
The objective of this paper is to examine the current role
of international accounting in the university curriculum
and to present recommendations for the internationalization
of the accounting curriculum.

Rueschhoff, Norlin G. "The Undergraduate International
Accounting Course." The Accounting Review, 47 (October

1972), 833-835.
The author states that the future of international accounting in the accounting curriculum rests at the undergraduate
level. He sees that the need for international accounting
is not to have a student of accounting specialize in a
regional area with emphasis on the economic and political
aspects of that specific area. Rather, international accounting instruction should train the professional accountant for the multinational corporation and its international
financial responsibilities.

Schoenfeld, Hanns-Martin. "International Influences on the
Contemporary Accounting Curriculum: International Accounting Instruction at the University of Illinois at Urbana-
Champaign." The International Journal of Accounting Education and Research, 10 (Fall 1974), 71-85.
The general educational philosophy utilized for development of a course on international accounting and the details
of the approach chosen are described.

Shields, Janice Christine. "Foreign Language and Accounting Expertise: A Marketable Combination." The International Journal of Accounting Education and Research, 17
(Fall 1981), 133-146.
The purpose of this article is to consider specifically the
benefits of and potential for combining foreign language
and accounting skills. The article concludes that in
today's business and accounting world, fluency in more than
one language is definitely a valuable asset.

AUTHOR INDEX

Abdeen, A., 128
Abdel-Magid, M.F., 146
Abdel-Malek, T., 79
Abs, H.J., 14
Adelberg, A.H., 47
Adler, M., 66, 79
Advani, R., 70
Agami, A.M., 14
Aggarwal, R., 14, 66, 140
Agmon, T., 66, 67
Alexander, M.O., 52
AlHashim, D.D., 5, 94, 146
Aliber, R.Z., 15
Alkier, M.A., 134
Altman, E.I., 133
Ameiss, A.P., 4, 154
Amernic, J.H., 56
Anderson, A.G., 67
Anderson, J.V.R., 56
Anderson, R., 47, 53
Ankrom, R.K., 79
Aranya, N., 56, 138
Armstrong-Flemming, N., 15
Arnold, J., 51
Arpan, J.S., 65, 97
Arthur, R.J., 101
Asselman, R.J., 132

Backer, M., 31
Baden, E.J., 32
Bailey, D.T., 149, 150
Bailey, R., 140
Bait-El-Mal, M.M., 146
Baker, H.K., 47
Baker, J.C., 14, 67
Ballinger, E., 61
Barbier, G., 134
Bardsley, R.G., 67
Barkas, J.M., 128
Barlev, B., 56
Barnett, J.S., 79
Barrack, J.B., 35
Barrett, M.E., 15, 47, 118, 134
Bartholomew, E.G., 56, 140
Bartlett, R.T., 5, 101
Baruch, H., 61
Basche, J., 61

Batt, W.F.J., 80
Bavishi, V.B., 47, 67
Bawly, D., 101
Baxter, W.J., 32, 118, 126
Beardsley, L.J., 67
Bedford, N.M., 140
Beecroft, K., 1
Beekhuizen, T., 136
Beidleman, C.R., 85
Belkaoui, A., 5
Belli, P., 65
Benjamin, J.J., 15, 61
Bennett, J.W., 67
Benoit, E., 1
Benson, H., 2, 6
Benston, G.J., 48
Bent, F.T., 133
Beresford, D.R., 32, 62
Berg, R., 101
Berry, M.H., 65
Bhushan, B., 80
Biagioni, L.F., 25
Bilson, J.F.O., 15
Binkowski, E., 101
Birati, A., 37
Black, F., 67
Blackshaw, I., 137
Blake, N., 138
Blausten, R., 141
Bloch, H.S., 68
Block, D.J., 62
Block, S.B., 30, 91
Blumberg, A., 82
Boersema, J., 125
Bond, J.D., 62
Booth, G.G., 16, 80
Bose, M., 118
Bostock, C., 53
Bougen, P., 35
Bourgeois, J.C., 7
Bourn, M., 32
Bowers, D.A., 80
Bradford, S.R., 15, 80
Bradley, D.G., 92
Bradley, G.E., 150
Bradman, E.A., 80
Bradt, J.D., 62
Branch, B., 32
Brantner, P.F., 101

Brealey, R.A., 139
Breen, F.G., 23
Brennan, W.J., 32
Brewer, T.L., 92
Briner, E.K., 56, 101
Briston, R.J., 32, 56, 129
Brittain, W.H.B., 16
Broke, A., 102
Brown, A., 53
Brown, J.G., 7
Brownell, P., 53
Brummet, R.L., 154
Buckley, A., 33
Buehler, V., 96
Burgert, R., 33
Burnett, R.A., 141
Burns, J.O., 97, 102, 154
Burt, J., 16

Cairns, D., 141
Calderon-Rossell, J.R., 81
Calhoun, D.A., 102
Calitri, J.C., 103
Callier, P., 81
Cargile, B., 42
Carmichael, D.R., 62
Carmichael, K., 103
Carroll, K.B., 114
Carstairs, R., 16
Castle, E.F., 48
Catherwood, F., 53
Chambers, R.J., 33, 122
Chan, K.H., 100, 103
Chandler, J.S., 131
Chang, D.L., 118
Chang, L.S., 48, 141
Chanhall, R.H., 47
Chastain, C.E., 53
Chastney, J.G., 2
Chazen, C., 62
Cheng, P.C., 118
Chetkovich, M.N., 6, 7
Chiu, J.S., 118
Choate, A.G., 103
Choi, F.D.S., 6, 16, 33, 48, 65, 68, 92, 119, 141
Chown, J., 103
Christie, A.J., 103
Christie, H., 137
Christofides, N., 16

Chu, J.M., 126
Cinnamon, A., 68
Clark, F.L., 17
Clark, R.S., 34
Clarke, F.L., 34
Clay, A.A., 154
Climo, T., 138
Coburn, D.L., 98
Cohn, R.A., 68
Collins, L., 134
Combes, J.H., 17
Comer, R.W., 34
Comiskey, E.E., 138
Compagnoni, A., 51
Connor, J.E., 17
Coombes, R.J., 34
Cooper, J.R.H., 17
Cooper, K., 17
Copeland, R.M., 17
Corbett, P.G., 6
Cornell, B., 17, 18, 80
Corsini, L., 60
Costouros, G.J., 135
Court, P., 56
Cowen, S.S., 98
Cowperthwaite, G.H., 6
Cracco, E., 133
Cretton, C., 104
Crum, W.F., 57
Cumby, R.E., 18
Cummings, J.P., 7
Cunningham, G.M., 71

DaCosta, R.C., 7, 68
Dale, B., 119
Dascher, P.E., 61, 154
Davey, N., 34
Davidson, A.G., 57
Davis, M., 104
Davis, S.I., 69
Dawson, S.M., 69
Deakin, B., 104
Deakin, E.B., 119
deBruyne, D., 7
deFaro, C., 71
de la Mahotière, S., 1, 143
Delap, R.L., 104
deMare, H.B., 136
Denis, J., 18

160

Denza, J., 34
Deupree, M.M., 18
Dev, S., 154
Devoe, R.J., 34
Dewhurst, J., 35
Dewhurst, R.F.J., 155
Dhaliwal, D.S., 48
Diamond, M.A., 95
Dietemann, G.J., 94
Dillard, J.F., 29, 61
Dilley, S., 104
Dodden, M.J., 155
Dorian, D.G., 129
Dreier, R., 105
Drury, D.H., 69, 125
Drury, J., 35
Duangploy, O., 18
DuBois, D.A., 119
Dufey, G., 20, 81
Dumas, B., 66, 79
Dykxhoorn, H., 57
Dyment, J.J., 69

Eaker, M.R., 75, 81, 82, 88
Earl, M., 19
Eddey, P.H., 34
Edey, H.C., 35
Edwards, J.D., 35
Edwards, J.R., 35
El-Adly, Y.A., 147
Elam, R., 98
El-Azma, M.A., 147
Elliott, E.L., 129
Ellis, J.K., 98
Elsea, C.A., 7
Emmanuel, C.R., 51
Enthoven, A.J.H., 2, 65, 129, 130
Errunza, V.R., 69, 126
Eun, C.S., 82
Evans, T.G., 19, 49, 71, 82
Everett, R.M., 82
Ewing, D.W., 1
Ezzamel, M.A., 52

Falk, H., 35, 147
Fantl, I.L., 19, 57, 98, 142
Farrag, S.M., 94
Feinschreiber, R., 105, 106, 107, 108
Fekrat, M.A., 19

Feldman, S.A., 8
Ferchat, R., 82
Ferris, K.R., 49
Feskoe, G., 82
Fielding, J., 36
Fieleke, N.S., 20
Filos, V.P., 134
Fincher, R.E., 62
Findlay, M.C., 69
Finney, M.J., 70, 108
Firth, M.A., 8, 49
Fisher, J., 68
Fisher, J., 36, 122
Fisk, C., 70
Fitzgerald, R.D., 8
Fleming, R., 36
Fletcher, J.W., 83
Flink, S.J., 37
Flint, D., 57
Flower, J., 20
Folks, W.R., 19, 70, 83
Foroughi, T.K., 130
Fotheringham, K.B., 83
Foutz, P.B., 155
Fowler, D.J., 98
Francis, J.R., 122
Franck, P., 83
Frank, W.G., 11
Fraser, D.R., 17
Fredrikson, E.B., 20
Frenkl, J.A., 20
Frey, K.M., 37, 84
Friedman, D., 84
Frishkoff, P., 136
Frumer, S., 147
Fujita, Y., 119
Fung, W.K.H., 70

Gabriel, P.P., 130
Gaertner, J.F., 8
Galbraith, J.K., 1
Gale, J.C., 128
Ganguli, G., 2
Garda, J.A., 94
Garman, M.B., 20
Gaskins, J.P., 108
Gautier, J.P., 140
Gehrke, J.A., 118
George, A.M., 82

Gibbs, M., 37
Gibson-Moore, D., 142
Giddy, I.H., 20, 21, 84
Gill, C.W., 37
Gilling, D.M., 122
Gniewosz, G., 123
Goch, D., 37
Goddard, C.S., 142
Goeltz, R.K., 71
Goettsche, H.G., 134
Goldstein, S.J., 73
Goodman, S.H., 84
Gorelik, G., 150
Graham, A.W., 123
Granow, W.W., 64
Gray, J.Y., 21
Gray, S.J., 8, 9, 49, 51, 52, 142
Green, A., 109
Green, J., 109
Green, W.H., 109
Greenleaf, J.A., 85
Gregor, W.T., 71
Grinyer, J., 37
Grollman, W.K., 57
Grossman, S.D., 15
Groves, R.E.V., 138, 142
Grundy, G., 23
Gull, D.S., 84
Gupta, S., 84
Guy, J.R.F., 71

Hackett, D.W., 61
Hadjinicolaou, Y., 136
Hallett, D., 71
Hammer, R., 109
Hampton, R., 9
Harding, M., 58
Harless, D.D., 110
Harrison, B.G., 123
Harvey, I., 9
Haslem, J.A., 47
Hauworth, W.P., 9, 38
Hayes, D.C., 49
Hayes, D.J., 9, 21
Heckerman, D., 84
Heenan, D.A., 93, 130
Heintz, J.A., 147
Heinz, P.D., 110
Helm, R.J., 74

Henaidy, H., 98
Herbert, L.J., 8
Hewins, R.D., 16
Hewson, J., 142
Hill, C., 142
Hill, D.J., 58
Hilley, J.L., 85
Hilliard, J.E., 21
Hilton, K., 52
Hinsey, J., 62
Hinton, P.R., 21
Hockey, P., 71
Hodges, S.D., 139
Holder, W.W., 51
Hole, R.C., 134
Hollis, M., 85
Holmes, G., 53, 125
Holt, R.N., 62
Holzer, H.P., 130, 131
Houghton, J.W., 17, 22
Houston, A.W., 38
Howard, F., 110
Howe, W.E., 9
Hoyt, N.H., 85
Hoyt, R.E., 150
Huang, R.D., 22
Huber, R.L., 126
Hughes, A., 110
Hugo, O., 46
Hunter, R.L., 71
Hussein, M.E., 9
Hussey, R., 53

Ichikawa, H., 120
Imai, Y., 85
Imdieke, L., 95
Inanga, E.L., 154
Ingram, R.W., 17
Ioannides, J.D., 110

Jackson, P.D., 22
Jacobi, M.H., 22
Jacque, L.L., 85
Jacquillat, B., 133
Jaggi, B.L., 50, 53, 131
Jagpal, H.S., 65
Jain, T.N., 118
James, G.F., 110
Jansz, R., 22

Jaruga, A.A., 151
Jay, D., 143
Jensen, H.L., 103
Johnson, H.G., 22
Johnston, D.J., 58
Johnston, T., 38
Jones, R.J., 93
Juchau, R., 47, 123
Jucker, J.V., 71

Kadet, J., 112
Kaen, F.R., 16, 80
Kafka, A., 131
Kahl, A., 5
Kahnamouyipour, H., 85
Kaikati, J., 62
Kanaga, W., 10
Katsuyama, S., 119
Kaye, R., 98
Keegan, W.J., 130
Kelley, P., 111
Kendall, D.M., 1
Kenley, W.J., 38
Kennedy, C., 38
Kern, W., 135
Kettell, B., 86
Kewin, A.H.E., 10
Keyserlingk, A.N., 58
Kim, S.H., 86, 98
Kim, S.H., 63
Kirby, J.C., 71
Kitching, J., 72
Klaassen, J., 136
Klein, J.R., 32
Klein, R.B., 22
Kleinschmidt, E.J., 69
Kline, J., 63
Knol, A.W., 136
Kobrin, S.J., 93
Kodama, A., 120
Kohlhagen, S.W., 20, 23, 86, 120, 12
Kolmin, F.W., 110
Kolmin, K.G., 115
Konrath, L.F., 23, 139
Koveos, P.E., 80
Kramer, G., 72
Kramer, J.L., 112
Kubin, K.W., 155
Kubota, K., 120

Kullberg, D.R., 58
Kupzhasar, N., 151
Kuzdrall, P.J., 86

Label, W.A., 62
Lafferty, M., 38, 143, 155
Lagae, J.P., 111
Lamond, R.A., 10
Lamp, W., 99, 111
Lange, C., 54
Lasusa, P.R., 86
Lawson, W.M., 7, 68
Lay, D.W., 39
Lee, B.E., 72
Lee, M., 58
Leech, S.A., 39
Lefebvre, C.J.L., 133
Leff, N.H., 65, 66
Leighton, G.R., 23
Lelievre, C.C., 131
Lelievre, T.W., 131
Lemke, K.W., 39
Lemon, W.M., 58
Leo, K., 23
Lessard, D.R., 66, 67, 72, 95
Lev, B., 147
Levasseur, M., 133
Levin, J.H., 72
Lewis, K.A., 23
Lieberman, G., 86
Lillie, J., 111
Lloyd, W.P., 73
Loeb, M., 152
Logue, D.E., 86
Lorange, P., 95
Lorensen, L., 24, 39
Louwers, P.C., 58
Lowe, H.D., 16
Loy, D., 24
Lück, W., 135
Lusztig, P., 90

MacKenzie, A., 10
Magat, W.A., 152
Magill, W.G.W., 39
Maher, M.W., 63
Maisonrouge, J.G., 2
Makin, J.H., 24, 87
Malkoff, A.R., 73

Malmstom, D., 99
Mann, M.H., 51
Mann, R.W., 59
Maples, L.D., 150
Markell, W., 59
Marriott, R.G., 39, 44
Marsh, H.L., 63
Marshall, A.J., 59
Mason, A.K., 10, 43
Mathur, I., 24, 87
Mattessich, R.V., 39
Maunders, K.T., 152
Mazzolini, R., 4, 73
McComb, D., 10, 54
McCosh, A.M., 40
McCosker, J.S., 93
McCrann, T., 123
McCrossin, F., 138
McDermott, J.E., 111
McEnally, R.W., 87
McFarlane, G., 143
McKee, T.E., 63
McKeon, A., 50
McKinnon, J., 40
McLean, A.T., 143
McMahon, T.J., 127
McMonnies, P.N., 10, 24, 25, 125, 143
McQueary, G.M., 63
Meagher, M.B., 22
Meckler, J.M., 89
Mehra, R., 73
Meins, P.G., 50
Meinster, D.R., 76
Mensah, Y.M., 25
Mepham, M.J., 127
Merrett, A.J., 40
Merten, A.G., 63
Merville, L.J., 99
Messier, W.F., 25
Messina, R.J., 88
Methven, P., 4
Micallef, J., 93
Milam, E.E., 2
Milano, D.R., 98
Miles, J.N., 11
Miles, M.A., 25
Miller, M.C., 52
Miller, S.W., 98
Mintz, S.M., 155

Mirus, R., 81
Mirza, A.M., 52
Mitchell, G.B., 40
Mitchell, K.R., 139
Moir, J.A.W., 40
Moir, R.J., 127
Monroe, W.F., 120
Moonitz, M., 59
Moore, D., 59
Moore, M.L., 103
Mora, R.E., 127
Morgan, J.R., 111
Morgan, R.G., 61
Morley, M.F., 50
Morpeth, D.S., 41
Morsicato, H.G., 95
Moser, S.T., 37
Most, K.S., 48, 54, 141
Motekat, U.K., 4, 14, 95, 152
Mueller, G.G., 3, 11, 50
Muis, J.W., 41
Mumford, M.J., 41
Munter, P., 25
Murdock, R.J., 29
Murenbeeld, M., 87
Murphy, G.J., 50
Myddleton, D.R., 41

Nackenson, C., 108
Nagy, R.J., 99
Naidu, G.N., 87
Nair, R.D., 11
Naumann-Etienne, R., 73
Needles, B.E., 12
Ness, W.L., 73, 112
Neuburger, H., 91
Neukomm, H.U., 88
Neumann, F.L., 58, 64
Newman, B., 112
Niehus, R.J., 135, 144
Nobes, C., 3, 12, 25, 110, 112, 144
Nordhauser, S.L., 112
Norgaard, C.T., 64
Norr, D., 26
Norwood, G.R., 119

Obersteiner, E., 74
Oblak, D.J., 74
Obstfeld, M., 18

O'Connor, W.F., 112
O'Doner, E.J., 62
O'Donovan, V., 144
Ogan, P., 131
O'Glove, T.L., 88
Ohno, N., 120
Oldfield, G.S., 86, 88
Oliver, D., 113
Oliver, M., 111
Olsen, B.N., 133
Olstein, R.A., 88
Owles, D., 12
Ozawa, T., 120

Page, N.B., 124
Pakkala, A.L., 26
Paraszczak, J., 152
Parker, J.W., 59
Parker, L.D., 50, 54
Parker, M.R., 88
Parker, R.H., 4, 124, 139, 144, 145
Parkes, H., 54
Parkinson, R.M., 26
Patz, D.H., 26
Pawliczek, R., 60
Paxson, D., 19
Peasnell, K.V., 41
Peckron, H.S., 113
Peña, P.A., 127
Percy, K., 37
Perera, M.H.B., 120
Periton, P., 145
Perlstein, P., 113
Perrin, J.R., 42
Peterson, A.F., 133
Petty, J.W., 99
Peyrard, J., 5
Phillips, J.D.W., 74
Pick, R.H., 51
Piper, A., 27
Plasschaert, S.R.F., 99
Platt, A., 42
Platt, W.H., 42
Pleak, R.E., 27
Pointon, L., 147
Polimeni, R.S., 27
Pollard, B.M., 122
Pomeranz, F., 12, 59
Portington, M., 27

Pratt, D.J., 39
Previts, G.J., 12
Price, C.I., 27
Price, L.N., 118
Prindl, A., 74
Pringle, J.J., 68

Qureshi, M., 3, 132

Radebaugh, L., 27, 28, 95, 128
Radford, R., 145
Radler, A.J., 113
Rankin, B.J., 24, 25
Rashkin, M.D., 113
Ravenscroft, D.R., 113, 114
Rayburn, F., 42
Rayman, R.A., 42
Raymond, R.H., 100
Reavell, F.M., 64
Reckers, P.M.J., 28
Redmayne, D.H., 59
Reichmann, T., 54
Reid, A., 104
Reinganum, M.R., 18
Reiss, J., 88
Remmers, H.L., 74
Ricchiute, D.N., 64
Rice, M.L., 87
Richards, F.E., 75
Richards, R.M., 17
Richards, W.R., 60
Rickard, D.R., 28
Rimlinger, F., 70
Risdon, M.P., 63
Robbins, S.M., 71, 75, 95, 96
Robertson, I.C.M., 60
Robertson, J., 55
Robishek, A.A., 75, 88
Robinson, C., 111
Robock, S.H., 2
Rodney, E., 96
Rodriguez, R.M., 28, 89
Rogalski, R.J., 28, 89
Rogers, W.L., 7
Rogness, E.C., 132
Rogow, R.B., 73
Romito, E.L., 114
Rosenfield, P., 28, 39, 42
Ross, R.S., 97

Rossitch, E., 89
Roy, J., 134
Rueschhoff, N., 8, 90, 155
Rummel, R.J., 93
Russo, S.M., 112
Rutenberg, D.P., 90
Ryan, E.D., 114
Ryder, F.R., 75

Sakakibara, E., 142
Sale, J.T., 42, 43, 114
Salkin, G.R., 16
Samuels, J.M., 142
Sangster, B.F., 75
Satubaldin, S., 152
Saunders, A., 76
Saville, R., 37
Savoie, L.M., 3
Sawicki, S.J., 153
Scapens, R.W., 42, 43
Schieneman, G.S., 12
Schlag, R.C., 114
Schmidt, D., 1
Schmitz, M.N., 114
Schmitz, W., 29
Schoenfeld, H.M., 135, 156
Schreuder, H., 55
Schwab, B., 90
Schwartz, B., 114
Schwartz, I., 13, 60
Schweikart, J.A., 5
Scorcey, M., 76
Scott, D.A., 29
Scott, G.M., 29, 96
Scott, M.R., 52
Seary, B., 145
Seghers, P.D., 115
Seidler, L.J., 29
Senbet, L.W., 69, 76
Serfass, W.D., 90
Severance, D.G., 63
Severn, A.K., 76
Shagam, J., 115
Shamis, G.S., 29
Shank, J.K., 29
Shapiro, A.C., 76, 77, 90, 93
Sharp, D., 100
Shaw, J.C., 43, 60
Shen, P., 77

Sherk, D.R., 121
Sherwin, J.T., 90
Sherwood, K.A., 55
Shetty, Y., 96
Shields, J.C., 156
Shin, T.S., 87
Shirley, R., 145
Shuaib, S.A., 132, 148
Shwayder, K.R., 30
Sibley, A., 30
Siegel, J.G., 51
Sim, A., 96
Simms, C.A., 115
Simon, S.H., 115
Singh, D.R., 121
Sinning, K.E., 57
Skerratt, L.C.L., 41
Smith, A.F., 30
Smith, C., 95, 119, 146, 154
Smith, C.W.D., 115
Smith, G.R., 135
Smith, W.A., 13
Soenen, L., 91
Solnik, B.H., 77, 78
Someya, K., 119
Spero, L., 15
Srinivasulu, S.L., 91
Spinks, N., 148, 149
Stamp, E., 43, 146
Standish, P.E.M., 43, 44
Stanley, M., 30, 91
Stansell, S.R., 83
Stanton, P.J., 122
Steinle, K., 30
Stern, M., 31
Stevenson, K.M., 44
Stewart, J.C., 100
Stickney, C.P., 15
Stillwell, M.I., 13
Stitt, C., 115
Stobaugh, R.B., 71, 75, 95, 96, 116
Stobie, B., 44
Stockton, K.J., 78, 91
Stokes, H.H., 91
Stoney, P., 32
Strawser, R.H., 154
Stulz, R.M., 78
Sumutka, A.R., 64
Sykes, A., 40

Symonds, E., 116

Tang, R.Y.W., 100
Tarrant, N., 146
Taylor, D., 44
Taylor, M.E., 28, 146
Teck, A., 31, 91
Tenz, W., 137
Thoman, G.R., 79
Thomas, R.D., 13
Tipgos, M.A., 60
Tomsett, E., 116
Tooman, L.D., 60
Torres, M., 128
Travers, N., 121
Treadwell, B.J., 121
Tremblay, D., 130
Trow, D.G., 44, 124
Tse, P.S., 97
Turk, I., 153
Turner, J.H., 78
Turner, J.N., 125
Tweedie, D.P., 44, 45, 55

Ungar, M., 37
Upson, R.B., 92

Van Agtmael, A.W., 94
Vancil, R.F., 40
Van Cise, J.G., 78
Van Den Bergh, R., 55
Van Rossem, J.P., 136
Van Seventer, A., 45
Van Valkenburg, M., 116
Vincent, G., 13
Vinso, J.D., 28, 89
Volten, H., 45, 137
Vuerings, R., 133

Wainman, D., 116
Walker, B.C., 29
Walker, E.W., 99
Walker, L.M., 11
Walker, R.G., 5
Walter, C.K., 100
Walton, H.C., 92
Wanless, P.T., 139
Wasley, R.S., 124
Watson, J., 78

Watt, G.C., 13
Wedley, W.C., 149
Weinstein, A.K., 60
Weinstein, S., 1
Wells, L.T., 55
Went, D., 148
Wentz, R.C., 92
Wesberry, J.P., 61
Westwick, C., 45, 46
White, B.J., 63
Whiteley, J., 132
Whitt, J.D., 128
Whittred, G.P., 124
Wihlborg, C., 92
Wilford, D.S., 25
Willey, R.W., 31
Willows, C., 4
Winfield, R.R., 46
Winjum, J.O., 139
Woelfel, C.J., 2
Wollstadt, R.D., 46
Woo, J.C.H., 46
Woodward, R.S., 76
Wooster, J.T., 79
Worthley, R.G., 16
Wortzel, L.H., 153
Wright, M.G., 55
Wu, F.H., 61, 100
Wündisch, K., 79
Wyman, H.E., 31, 47
Wynn, R., 32

Yahalomi, B., 147
Yamakawa, T.T., 121
Yang, C.L., 153
Yost, G.J., 116, 117
Young, A., 83
Yung, S.Y.T., 122

Zappala, F.J., 137
Zeff, S., 46, 124, 128

JOURNALS RESEARCHED

1. Abacus (Australia)
2. Accountancy (England)
3. The Accountant (England)
4. The Accountant's Magazine (Scotland)
5. Accounting and Business Research (England)
6. The Accounting Review
7. The Australian Accountant (Australia)
8. Business International
9. CA Magazine (Canada)
10. The CPA Journal
11. The Chartered Accountant in Australia (Australia)
12. Columbia Journal of World Business
13. Financial Analysts Journal
14. Financial Executive
15. Financial Management
16. The Financial Review
17. Harvard Business Review
18. Internal Auditor
19. International Executive
20. The International Journal of Accounting Education and Research
21. The International Tax Journal
22. Journal of Accountancy
23. Journal of Accounting and Economics
24. Journal of Accounting, Auditing and Finance
25. Journal of Accounting Research
26. The Journal of Business
27. Journal of Business Finance and Accounting (England)
28. Journal of Contemporary Business
29. The Journal of Finance
30. Journal of Financial and Quantitative Analysis
31. Journal of International Business Studies
32. Management Accounting
33. Management International Review (West Germany)
34. Sloan Management Review
35. The Woman CPA

Heterick Memorial Library
Ohio Northern University

DUE	RETURNED	DUE	RETURNED
1.		13.	
2.		14.	
3.		15.	
4.		16.	
5.		17.	
6.		18.	
7.		19.	
8.		20.	
9.		21.	
10.		22.	
11.		23.	
12.		24.